THAT'S
IN THE
BIBLE?
≈≈≈

The Ultimate
Learn-As-You-Play
Bible Quizbook

THAT'S
IN THE
BIBLE?
≈≈≈

The Ultimate
Learn-As-You-Play
Bible Quizbook

WICK ALLISON

A DELL BOOK

Published by
Dell Publishing
a division of Bantam Doubleday Dell Publishing Group, Inc.
1540 Broadway
New York, New York 10036

Portions of this book appeared originally in *Reader's Digest*.

ISBN 0-440-50690-5

Printed in the United States of America

For Virgilio Levi
Friend, mentor, and example

ACKNOWLEDGMENTS

The inspiration and format of this book I owe to my wife, Christine Allison, whose invitation to collaborate informally on her article "Is *That* in the Bible?" for *Reader's Digest* reignited my lifelong interest in the King James Version and in the Bible itself. John Boswell believed that the resulting discoveries could be built upon and expanded into a book—and insisted that it be done. Patty Brown made sure it was. Emily Reichert enthusiastically adopted the project, and Steve Ross pushed it to fruition. I thank them all. I would also like to add a word of appreciation to the Reverend Howard Hedges of Plymouth Park Methodist Church in Dallas and the Reverend Mitchell Pacwa, S.J., of Loyola University in Chicago for their counsel and advice. The mistakes remain my own.

CONTENTS

INTRODUCTION

How This Book Can Help You Read, Enjoy, and Learn More from the Bible

≈≈≈

THE BIBLE CAN BARELY BE READ IN ONE YEAR, LET ALONE IN one sitting. And its complexity and richness certainly can't be comprehended in one reading. The Bible merits study, and study requires guidance. But while there are plenty of Bible guides and literally thousands of books of commentary available to anyone who wants them, the plain fact is that most of us don't. While we may be interested in learning more about the Bible, few of us aim to become scholars or amateur theologians. We want a grasp of the central characters and we want guideposts to mark the essential points we need to remember and understand.

This quizbook is designed to help you read the Bible. Our hope is that it will deepen both your pleasure in and knowledge of the Bible. To help accomplish this, it is organized into the same sections as the Bible itself, so that you or your study group can follow it in sequence with the Bible. There are no trick questions in this book (although some *are* tricky!). Every question and every answer has been designed to help you increase your knowledge of the Bible. In addition, the answers are designed for discussion purposes, making the answers as integral to your study as the questions.

The Bible continues to be far and away the best-selling book in the world. In the United States alone it sells 15 to 16 million copies a year. By comparison, the top best-seller on the hardcover list as I write has sold 1.6 million copies. The best-selling paperback has sold 4.2 million copies. Next year both these books will be forgotten, so there is no reason to even mention their names. But the Bible sells at a consistent rate of three to five times that amount *every year*.

Reviewing these astoundingly high sales figures for the Bible, an executive with the Christian Booksellers Association asked me rhetorically (and plaintively), "Where do they all go?" Another and perhaps more important question is, "Why do people want to read the Bible?" Or in the case where it is being bought as a gift for someone else, "Why do people think other people need to read the Bible?"

For believers, the answer is quite simple, but for everyone else it's not. For nonbelievers, for semibelievers, for wanna-be believers, for the curious, for the doubters, for the once-agnostic-but-not-so-sure, for the pained and hurting, for the good seeking a definition of good, for the bad seeking a way out of bad, for the dispirited seeking spirit, for the disinherited seeking a home, for the libertine seeking restraint and the constrained seeking liberty, for the altar boy who became an inside trader, for the Sunday School teacher who's four times divorced, for the teenager crying over an abortion and for the boyfriend who told her to do it—for all of weak and vacillating and immoral mankind, this book continues as a Blessing, a salve on the wound of conscience and a stairway to a better life.

Why does the Bible have so many readers? Because in this book God talks to people exactly like us.

Abraham is a Patriarch. But is that the same Abraham who was willing to have his wife sleep with someone else if it will save his skin? Israel continues the Covenant. But isn't that Israel the same Jacob who deceived his father to get his blessing? Peter will publicly pronounce the good news on Pentecost and later die a martyr's death. But isn't that the Simon Peter who took the coward's way out by denying Christ? Aren't we all at some point in our lives compromisers, liars, cowards?

Where is the perfect person among us? He doesn't exist. But in the Bible we find that all this imperfection is to a purpose. Perfection is promised, and perfection comes. And it is so radically different from how imperfect people conceived what perfection should be that it is slaughtered.

Someone has said that the Bible is a book with a thousand heartbeats. It throbs with life. With a keen eye to human behavior and with an ear that hears every false note, it reports the pathetic dispassionately and sweeps us up to the sublime with sparse words. This is a book that sees no problem in boring its reader with bureaucratic number crunching in one section before encountering a talking ass in another. More interestingly, this is a book that tells without embarrassment the worst stories about its greatest heroes. It is frank. It is often funny. And in many, many places it is poetry.

WHY I USE THE KING JAMES VERSION

The King James Version is not only outmoded in its language but outdated in its scholarship. (Koine Greek, in which most of the New Testament is written in the earliest manuscripts, wasn't understood by the King James translators, who used ancient Greek as best they could. Their best, as we shall see, was very good.)

In spite of its admitted limitations, I use the King James Version for two reasons. One, it is still the best-selling translation of the Bible and thus the Bible most people encounter and read; therefore its phrasing is the most familiar to the greatest number of people. Two, the grace and beauty of the Elizabethan writing rings with surer authority than any translation that has come since. This is why the King James Version is the only *translation* to be ranked among the world's classics of literature.

On the question of authenticity, I turn to Reynolds Price, author of *A Palpable God*, who made his own translations of thirty passages from the Old and New Testaments. After learning Koine and closely reading the Latin Vulgate (which is close to being a primary source itself, since St. Jerome relied on manuscripts no longer in existence), Reynolds came to the conclusion that the King James Version holds truer to the original texts. He uses an incident recorded in Mark 5 to show why.

Jesus enters a house where there is a great wailing because the young daughter of the homeowner has

ERRANT BIBLES

The effort to publish a suitable English translation of the Bible was not without its pitfalls. Here are some of the more famous missteps.

Edition	Date	Nickname	Why It's Called That
Geneva Bible	1560	Breeches Bible	Genesis 3:7 reads, "They sewed fig leaves together and made themselves breeches." Unlikely.
Geneva Bible	1562	Placemakers Bible	Matthew 5:9 reads, "Blessed are the placemakers."
Bishops Bible	1568	Treacle Bible	Jeremiah 8:22 asks, "Is there no treacle in Gilead?" (Gilead was famous for its balm.)
Douay-Rheims	1610	Rosin Bible	Its first edition had Jeremiah ask, "Is there no rosin in Gilead?"
Bishops Bible	1632	Wicked Bible	Dropping an important word makes the 7th commandment read, "Thou shalt commit adultery."
King James	1702	Printers Bible	Instead of "princes" in Psalm 119, this edition reads, "Printers have persecuted me without cause."

died. Jesus says no, she's only asleep, which causes the mourners to jeer at him until he walks over to her and tells her to wake up, which she does. In the King James Version, "he cometh into the house of the ruler of the synagogue and seeth the tumult" (Mark 5:38).

Note that Jesus *sees*. This is a physical act. Price points out that in the original languages the Bible is "unremittingly physical, like most other sane human narrations." That is, action follows cause, and cause usually arises from an act of the senses, from a physical perception of some sort. "Failure to confront that reality," Price writes, "is failure to tell the story, failure to confront and recreate (in a language like English, equally capable of the reality) the embarrassing and demanding corporeality of the original."

Yet most contemporary translations cannot pass this simple test, as Mark 5 shows. The *New English Bible* says he "found a great commotion." The *New American Bible* says he "was struck" by the noise. The *Jerusalem Bible* and *J. B. Phillips* say "Jesus noticed." None of these is as direct or as convincing as the plain fact that with his own eyes Jesus *sees* the despair of the grieving family.

The translators of the King James Version, we need to remember, lived in a world technologically closer to the original writers than ours. Life was earthier and less abstract, and language follows life. Maybe their translation reeks with the same smells as the original because they were smelling the same smells.

But that's not the only reason for its popularity. The King James Version is itself a triumph of the English language. To take only one example, let's look at Matthew 6:28–29; in one of the most "modern" editions, *The Bible in Today's English*, it is translated as:

And why worry about clothes? Look at how the wild flowers grow: they do not work or make clothes for themselves. But I tell you that not even King Solomon with all his wealth had clothes as beautiful as one of these flowers.

Now listen to the rendering from the King James Version:

Why take ye thought for raiment? Consider the lilies of the field,
how they grow; they toil not, neither do they spin: Yet I say unto you,
That Solomon in all his glory was not arrayed like one of these.

No wonder the King James Version echoes through-out English literature, from Milton to Faulkner to Toni Morrison, with an authority and a resonance un-matched in the language.

Of the modern translations, I recommend the *New International Version*. Although it is an entirely new translation from the original Hebrew, Aramaic, and Greek texts, its sponsors made a wise decision in re-taining the language and style of the King James Ver-sion in the most familiar passages while correcting its many archaisms and bringing the vocabulary up to date. While it does not match the majesty of the King James Version, and at times falls far short of duplicat-ing its cadence, it is the best attempt so far.

A HISTORY OF THE COVENANTS

The Bible (from *Biblia*, books) could be retitled *The History of the Covenants*, and if we use the synonym *testament* for covenant, we can see that it already has been. The Old Testament records the first covenant with Noah and then the great covenant with Abraham, which will last with his seed forever. In the Law, in its histories, in its songs, and in its prophecies, it tells of the faith in the covenant, the abuses against it, the punishments, and the pleadings for redemption. In the New Testament the promises of the Old are fulfilled, and at the Last Supper a new and everlasting covenant is made.

The word "testament" comes to us from the Latin *testes* or testicles. It derives from the ancient Near Eastern custom of placing one's hand on the other party's testicles in making a solemn pledge, conveying not only the trust of the two parties but also that the pledge is binding on the future generations that will come from the seed of each man. We see this custom in two literal instances in Genesis. Abraham in his old age sends his eldest servant back to Haran to find a wife for his son Isaac. Before the servant leaves, Abraham requires that he "put his hand under the thigh . . . and sware" (Gen 24:9). Two generations later when Jacob is dying, he calls for his son Joseph and says to him, ". . . put, I pray thee, thy hand under my thigh . . ." (Gen 47:29). *The Bible in Today's English* translates Jacob's request less euphemistically as "put your hand between my thighs."

When God made the great Covenant with Abraham (Gen 15), he employed another ancient custom, known as "cutting a covenant," in which parties to the agreement would cut a sacrificial animal into two parts and walk between them. In this case one party—God—who is symbolized by a "smoking furnace and a burning lamp" passes between the animals Abraham has placed on the altar, perhaps reflecting that this is an unconditional covenant on God's part, regardless of what Abraham does or doesn't do.

As the Covenant undergoes renewal under Moses, it becomes more explicit and more detailed. Some scholars, including Meredith Kline in *The Treaty of the Great King*, maintain that the Ten Commandments and most of Deuteronomy are written in the style of ancient treaties, examples of which have now been unearthed on clay tablets in recent excavations. There is a preamble recounting the authority of the power making the treaty ("I am the Lord your God, Who brought you out of the land of Egypt"), a prologue describing the previous history of the relationship, stipulations and oaths, and instructions for implementing the treaty. This argument seems logical enough, and it is helpful in understanding the particular formulations used in the Mosaic law. Also, the Code of Hammurabi (ca. 1790 B.C.) gives an example of a working legal system in the ancient world where case law has been compiled over a hundred- or two-hundred-year period to guide judges in making decisions. While there are many similarities between Mosaic law and the Babylonian code which precedes it by about three hundred years, as might be expected between societies related racially and culturally, the Babylonian code and other legal "documents" of the period are almost exclusively civil. The Mosaic law, on the other hand, is almost exclusively religious and moral, codifying as it does a preexisting Covenant between God and his Chosen People.

ABOUT DATING AND AUTHORSHIP

The questions of who wrote the books of the Bible and when they wrote them are difficult to answer with precision. From the late nineteenth century until a generation ago, the New Testament was generally dated much later than it is today. While the continuing debate shifts half a decade here and there, until new evidence is found it seems that the Gospel of St. Mark was written in the early to middle sixties by a disciple of Peter (who was martyred in A.D. 64) by the name of John Mark. The book was written for a Roman readership, as shown by its Latinisms in certain passages, and contains Aramaic expressions which betray a Palestinian background. Matthew and Luke, the two other Synoptic gospels, are commonly placed after A.D. 70. Matthew and Luke rely on Mark and seemingly also rely on another common source, which scholars have labeled the "Q Document." Matthew contains many passages of the sayings of Jesus, most notably the Sermon on the Mount and the parables, which are unique to it and which have led to scholarly speculation that an early Aramaic version was compiled by the Apostle Matthew perhaps twenty to thirty years before the gospel named after him reached its final form. The Gospel of St. John seems almost certainly to have been written before A.D. 90, and because of discoveries at Qumran, where the Dead Sea Scrolls were found, some scholars now speculate that it was written much earlier, perhaps as early as A.D. 40. (For further discussion, see Chapter 6.) Its source was St. John, who seems to be "the beloved disciple" (although it's never clearly stated in the gospel) and who was therefore the eyewitness on which the account relies, although the principal author may have been a disciple of John who acted as scribe and biographer.

The Old Testament, or more specifically the Pentateuch, has been subjected to intense scrutiny. Textual critics have identified five strands of writing in these five books: J, who seems to have written in the tenth century B.C. and whose initial comes from *Yahweh*, the name he employs for God (or *Jahweh* in the German spelling; *Jehovah* in earlier English renderings); E, or the Elohist, for *Elohim*—the plural name he used for God—who added considerable material in Genesis, Exodus, and Numbers; P, for the Priest or priestly school who wrote nearly all of Leviticus and the first account of Creation in Genesis; D, for the author of most of Deuteronomy; and R, for the Redactor, who performed the final editing that brought the five strands together. These strands are clearly visible in many cases, even to the layman—especially J, who is a vivid portrayer of character with an elliptic style and a sure instinct for the telling detail.

But the theory of the five strands, while coherent, leaves much unexplained. For example, it is clear that some passages are of very ancient origin, pre-Davidic and even pre-Mosaic, especially the great blessing (Num 6:24) and the "song of Deborah" (Judg 5:7). Stripped of the passages before and after it, Jacob's account of seeing God "face to face" (Gen 32:24–30) is extremely primitive, perhaps rubbed down to its essentials by countless retellings from generation to generation. Also, it seems unlikely that even such a sophisticated and educated culture as Solomon's Israel would have known of ancient practices which are clearly reflected in the Mosaic law and which, as we have seen, have only recently come to light through archeological discoveries. If J and E are dated correctly in the Solomonic or post-Solomonic era, they are as far removed in time from those ancient practices as we are from Christopher Columbus, in the case of Moses, or the Dark Ages, in the case of Abraham.

We are confronted with an even greater problem. Our contemporary ideas of historical evidence, sequential dating, individual ownership—not to mention individual creativity—are hopelessly distant from a tribal society whose collective memory retained in chants and stories its (mostly) unembellished ancestral record. That this record is ascribed to Moses, who liberated and refreshed it by liberating and restoring the tribe, and who undoubtedly during forty years in the desert contributed his portion to it, should not strike any objective person as unusual. (We routinely ascribe to our Founding Fathers ideas on political liberty which originated with Locke, Montesquieu, and the ancient Greeks.) What would be unusual would be for a tribal nation to wait a thousand years for writers to invent its history for it.

It seems once again, as in the case of the New Testament, that tradition may be more reliable than scholarship was once willing to concede. From these books we know more with greater authority about the founding of the Jewish people through the great covenant with Abraham and his progeny than we know about the founding of Rome and its early history fourteen hundred years later.

HOW TO USE THIS BOOK AS A BIBLE STUDY GUIDE

This book can be used either as a simple quizbook to test your Bible knowledge or as a study guide to follow in reading and learning about the Bible in greater depth.

As a quizbook it's fairly simple. By keeping track of your correct answers, you will be able to measure your comprehension and retention of key Biblical facts. A knowledgeable student of the Bible ought to be able to answer 90 percent of the questions in each section correctly; the novice can use the questions and answers as touchstones of information and deeper exploration of the relevant sections.

As a study guide, the book is divided into chapters following the canonical organization of the Bible. At the beginning of each chapter, a short introduction to the books is followed by recommended readings and a quiz. At the end of the book, the answers to the quiz questions are given, and where appropriate, before the answer a specific reading is recommended, which the answer then explicates or expands on, citing specific chapter and verse.

The purpose of this book is to make the reading of the Scriptures enjoyable while being educational, but the responsibility lies with the reader to stop at each answer, read the relevant scriptural passage, and reflect on its meaning, using the answer as a supplemental aid to reflection. Some answers are short; some are almost self-explanatory. Others place the person or event into the larger context of the story of salvation. While there is only one "correct" answer to each question, there can be as many interpretations of that answer as there are readers (which, come to think of it, is why we have so many denominations). A discussion group under the guidance of an experienced teacher is always the best way to study the Bible and to ferret out from under its many layers of meaning the best understanding of its underlying message.

There have been many collections of questions and answers about the Bible, and there will be many more. Some are fun and games; others seem intent on tripping up their readers on minor characters or irrelevant numbers (who cares how long the second oldest man in Genesis lived?). The point of this edition is different. Its mission is to entertain you for a reason, and that is to deepen your understanding of the story of Redemption as revealed to us by the great gift of this Good Book.

The Bible is the place where the human and the divine meet, where they speak to one another, clash, irritate each other, and fall in love. Welcome to it, and have fun.

—Wick Allison

The Books of the Old Testament

Genesis
Exodus
Leviticus
Numbers
Deuteronomy
Joshua
Judges
Ruth
1 Samuel
2 Samuel
1 Kings
2 Kings
1 Chronicles
2 Chronicles
Ezra
Nehemiah
Esther
Job
Psalms
Proverbs
Ecclesiastes
The Song of Solomon
Isaiah
Jeremiah
Lamentations
Ezekiel
Daniel
Hosea
Joel
Amos
Obadiah
Jonah
Micah
Nahum
Habakkuk
Zephaniah
Haggai
Zechariah
Malachi

The Books of the New Testament

Matthew
Mark
Luke
John
The Acts
Romans
1 Corinthians
2 Corinthians
Galatians
Ephesians
Philippians
Colossians
1 Thessalonians
2 Thessalonians
1 Timothy
2 Timothy
Titus
Philemon
Hebrews
James
1 Peter
2 Peter
1 John
2 John
3 John
Jude
Revelation

CHAPTER 1

HOW WELL DO YOU KNOW THE GOOD BOOK?

≈≈≈

This INTRODUCTORY QUIZ IS A WARM-UP. IF YOU ARE FAIRLY familiar with the Bible, you ought to answer at least 23 of the 25 questions correctly. If you are coming back to the Bible after a long absence or if the whole experience is new to you, be lenient with yourself, although you'll probably be surprised how well you do with a well-considered guess.

Answers begin on page 137.

1. The most frequently mentioned woman in the Bible is:

a. Eve   c. The Virgin Mary
b. Sarah   d. Rachel

2. The most frequently mentioned man, after Jesus himself, in the Bible is:

a. David   c. Moses
b. Abraham   d. Paul

3. The longest book in the Bible is:

a. Jeremiah   c. Ezekiel
b. Genesis   d. Psalms

4. The shortest book in the Bible is:

a. Second Epistle of John   c. Epistle to Philemon
b. Obadiah   d. Nahum

5. The shortest verse in the Bible is

_____.

6. The shortest prayer in the Bible is

_____.

7. The Old Testament book most often referred to or quoted in the New Testament is:

a. Psalms   c. Daniel
b. Isaiah   d. Genesis

BIBLE STATS

Number of words (total):	845,000
Number of words in the Old Testament	647,000
Number of words in the New Testament	198,000
Number of verses (total):	31,173
Number of verses in the Old Testament	23,214
Number of verses in the New Testament	7,959

8. What New Testament book relies on the most Old Testament books?

a. Matthew
b. Luke

c. Epistle to the Hebrews
d. Revelation

9. Among the "lost" books mentioned in the Bible but not included in it is:

a. Book of Jasher
b. Book of Baruch

c. Book of Zephaniah
d. Book of Judith

10. The Hebrew Bible does not include among the Prophets which of these books:

a. Isaiah
b. Jeremiah

c. Ezekiel
d. Daniel

11. After the books of the four major prophets come the writings of the so-called minor prophets. How many minor prophets are there?

a. four
b. seven

c. ten
d. twelve

12. The Book of Lamentations is included among the Prophetic Books of the Bible, even though it is not a prophecy, because it is thought to have been written by:

a. Isaiah
b. Jeremiah

c. Ezekiel
d. Daniel

13. What is the only book in the Bible that does not mention God?

14. The longest reign of any king in the Bible is by:

a. David   c. Manasseh
b. Solomon   d. Hezekiah

15. The shortest reign of any king in the Bible is by:

a. Saul   c. Herod Agrippa I
b. Asa   d. Zimri

16. Which two books in the Bible begin with "In the beginning . . ."?

17. What book of the Bible is a collection of five smaller books?

18. What is the most often used noun in the Bible:

a. Lord   c. water
b. Israel   d. wilderness

19. What is currently considered by scholars to be the oldest complete book of the Bible?

a. Judges   c. Exodus
b. Second Samuel   d. Deuteronomy

20. What is currently considered to be the latest book written?

a. Revelation   c. Epistle to the Hebrews
b. Gospel of John   d. Second Epistle of Peter

21. Who is traditionally believed to have written the first five books of the Bible?

a. Joshua   c. Ezra
b. Moses   d. Aaron

CHAPTER AND VERSE

The Bible wasn't divided in chapters until circa A.D. 1200, when Stephen Langton, the Archbishop of Canterbury, first incorporated chapter divisions in the Latin Vulgate. His divisions didn't always follow the sense of the text, but they are used mostly in their original form to this day. In 1551 Robert Estienne, printer to Francis I of France, first included verse numbers in an edition of the Greek New Testament. The Geneva Bible in 1560 was the first to include chapter and verse divisions for the entire Bible.

22. The Old Testament is, among other things, a history of the Hebrews. But two books have non-Hebrews as their main characters. Which are they?

23. Over fifty authors, some well known and some anonymous, contributed to the sixty-six books of the Bible, but one author is responsible for more books than any other single person. Who?

24. The Bible begins at the dawn of Creation and ends with the prophecy of the End Times. Which book of the Bible spans more time than all other sixty-five books put together?

25. The very last word of the Bible is _____. (Don't peek. Think about it.)

CHAPTER 2

THE PENTATEUCH

≈≈≈

Peruse the books of philosophers with all their
pomp of diction. How meager, how contempt-
ible are they when compared with the Scriptures!

—JEAN JACQUES ROUSSEAU

THE FIRST FIVE BOOKS OF THE BIBLE ARE THE PENTATEUCH
(from the Greek *penta*, five, and *teuchos*, scroll). They
are also known as the Books of Moses and make up
the written Torah of the Jewish tradition. They re-
count the history of the first Covenants from the Creation, through the origin of the Jewish race with Abraham, to the death of Moses.

Of the five books, *Genesis* stands as one of the great
literary and spiritual classics of all civilization. Like
any classic, this book must be read over and over
again for the reader to enter into some of its more
elliptical passages, which capture with startling
abruptness characters as rich and complex as any to
be found in Shakespeare or Dickens. Original sin,
committed in the Garden of Eden, sprouts up every-
where, even among the noblest of the Patriarchs. Mur-

der, lust, jealousy, drunkenness, prostitution, boastfulness, and thievery lurk on every other page as mankind, a newly formed and therefore awkward actor, stumbles to play its part in the great story of Redemption.

The reader will encounter in Genesis two different stories of the creation of Adam, two accounts of the numbers of animals taken on the Ark, two stories of the Covenant with Abraham, and many other repetitions known among scholars as "doublets." The fact that these passages parallel and often complement one another show the antiquity of the sources; the variations should only be expected in an oral tradition. That they remain after the oral was transposed to the written demonstrates the sacredness with which the traditions were held, since no effort was made later to make them agree. This is called by historians the "test of embarrassment." If the text had been concocted out of whole cloth, no doubt it would be much less confusing and much more logical in its presentation, without internal contradictions and conflicting accounts. The problems in Genesis, in the historian's view, are a testimony to its authenticity.

Exodus is the great tribal epic of liberation, its main role occupied by Moses, one of history's great personalities, at first impetuous and dangerous, next reluctant and stammering, and transformed again to be both patient and decisive. As Daniel Russ has pointed out, unlike the legendary and even fantastical origins of Sumerian, Greek, Roman, and European epics, Exodus is grounded in characters, events, and practices that are humanly possible and therefore historically probable. But it is more than history; it is an interpretation of history, of why things happened the way they did. And it is at the same time an instruction for the future, with the rite of the Passover and the Ten Commandments presenting the tribe with obligations which they must never forget.

Leviticus is the Book of the Levites, or the priestly tribe of Israel. It lays out the detailed social and religious code by which Israel is to be governed. Its purpose is to purge the people of their paganism by making God's presence among them the center of daily life. The people had spent four hundred years in Egypt and were corrupted by Egyptian practices and superstitions, as the incident of the Golden Calf in Exodus shows. (One commentator noted that it may have taken God only one night to get Israel out of Egypt, but it took forty years to get Egypt out of Israel.)

Numbers (named for the census taken at Sinai) is better titled in Hebrew as *Bemidbar* or "In the Wilderness." This is the book of the years of wandering after God enters his punishment on the people for their disloyalty. It has also been called "The Book of Murmurings," and for a good reason, because it is permeated with the seething discontent of a people condemned to die in the desert before seeing the promised land.

Deuteronomy ("The Second Law") is mainly taken up with Moses' final addresses to the people, expanding on the Ten Commandments and preparing them to enter finally into the Promised Land. It ends with a beautiful eulogy to the great prophet "whom the Lord knew face to face."

The Mosaic religion as set down in the Pentateuch became the embodiment of the nation. It is at times primitive and at times sophisticated but it is never

---

DID ADAM EAT AN APPLE?

Genesis doesn't say. The apple's association with the fruit of the tree of knowledge in the Garden of Eden may have arisen from a confusion of the Latin *malum*, or evil, with *malus*, apple tree. The fruit is more likely to have been a pomegranate or a fig.

---

stylized. Sometimes it is so vivid in its portrayals that the distant past becomes alive, and we are there as Abraham bargains with God to save Sodom or Judah dallies with a wayside prostitute who turns out to be his daughter-in-law or Moses tries without success to rid himself of the divine commission. Whatever tests the historians may devise, the final proof of its authenticity is its realism and its consistent note of surprise at the vagaries of human nature.

SELECTED READINGS:
Genesis 1–9, 11–35, 37–50; Exodus 1–19, 31–34; Leviticus 16, 19–20 ("The Holiness Code"); Numbers 9–16, 20–25, 31; Deuteronomy 6, 29–34.

Answers begin on page 139.

MEMORABLE COMMENTS

1. God cursed Adam for eating of the tree of knowledge, saying he was:

a. ingratitude incarnate
b. the bane of his existence
c. dust, and unto dust he would return
d. biting the hand that fed him

2. When Cain was confronted by God, who inquired somewhat suspiciously as to the whereabouts of his brother Abel, he replied:

a. The road to hell is paved with good intentions.
b. Blood is thicker than water.
c. Am I my brother's keeper?
d. The devil take the hindmost!

3. After Joseph was reunited with his brothers, he asked permission of Pharaoh to bring his family to Egypt. Pharaoh readily agreed, saying they could live off:

a. the sweat of their brows
b. the fat of the land

THE SEVEN FAT YEARS

Congress, take note. When Joseph became governor of Egypt, he imposed a tax of only 20 percent on the produce of the land—with the result that he "gathered corn as the sand of the sea, very much, until he left numbering, for it was without number" (Gen 41:49). By encouraging such productivity, Egypt survived the seven lean years that followed. Who says the Bible isn't relevant?

c. the fruit of the vine
d. the sheaves of the fields

4. Moses grew up as a Prince of Egypt, but after killing an Egyptian in defense of a fellow Hebrew, he fled to Midian where he married and declared himself:

a. rooted to the spot
b. a stranger in a strange land
c. shorn like a lamb
d. free at last

5. When Moses and Aaron approached Pharaoh, they quoted the Lord God, saying:

a. There is a tide in the affairs of men.
b. Time is of the essence.
c. Let my people go.
d. Let slip the dogs of war.

6. When the pagan soothsayer Balaam went up on the mountain to curse the Israelites, he saw their great numbers and exclaimed:

a. What hath God wrought!
b. Jumping Jehoshaphat!
c. Holy Moses!
d. Angels defend us!

FAMOUS PEOPLE

7. According to Genesis, the entire human race flowed from Adam. But not everyone was a part of this direct descent. Who was not a part of the direct line?

a. Seth   c. Noah
b. Cain   c. Enoch

8. When he sent Cain into exile, the Lord placed a mark on his forehead so all would know he was:

a. a murderer   c. an outcast
b. protected   d. cursed

9. Since it is the story of the Creation, Genesis contains a lot of firsts. Match the first with the appropriate person (with so few people and so many firsts, there can be multiple answers).

____Noah	a.	First city builder
____Abel	b.	First hunter
____Cain	c.	First shepherd
____Nimrod	d.	First farmer
____Shechem	e.	First shepherdess
____Abraham	f.	First priest
____Rachel	g.	First altar builder
____Lamech	h.	First drunk
____Melchizedek	i.	First polygamist
____Naamah	j.	First daughter mentioned
____Tubalcain	k.	First prophet
____Lot	l.	First craftsman
____Enoch	m.	First bargainer

n. First to commit incest
o. First to be assumed into
   heaven
p. First rapist

10. When Sarah overheard the Lord tell Abraham that she would soon conceive a child, she:

a. fell on her knees in thanksgiving   c. laughed
b. fainted   d. wept

11. Laban pursued Jacob after he left his territory because he believed Jacob had stolen:

a. all his goods
b. his daughter Rachel
c. his household gods
d. his cattle and sheep

12. Jacob spent the night before he was to confront his brother, Esau, and his "welcome-home" committee of 400 armed men:

a. praying to the Lord for deliverance
b. preparing defenses around his camp
c. dallying with his concubines
d. wrestling with an assailant

13. Laban was not entirely innocent himself. He had tricked Jacob into marrying his daughter:

a. Rachel   c. Rebekah
b. Leah   d. Judith

14. Tricks abound in Genesis. Match the trickster with the person tricked. (Warning: In some cases the

---

MOSES WAS A JEW, RIGHT?

Wrong. The twelve sons of Jacob, or Israel, were Reuben, Simeon, Levi, Judah, Zebulen, Issachar, Dan, Gad, Asher, Naphtali, Joseph, and Benjamin. Moses and his brother Aaron were Levites, or descendants of Levi. The descendents of Judah became known as Jews. It is not recorded what the descendents of Reuben were known as.

---

tricksters are incorrigible, so there can be multiple answers.)

I. Abraham_____	a. Shechem
II. Jacob_____	b. Benjamin
III. Rachel_____	d. Abimelech
IV. Joseph_____	e. Judah
V. Simeon_____	f. Isaac
VI. Tamar_____	g. Laban
	h. Pharaoh

15. The Covenant was originally made with one family, to be passed as a blessing from father to son. Which of these Patriarchs was *not* in the line of inheritance?

a. Israel   c. Joseph
b. Isaac   d. Judah

16. Fertility was very important if the blessing was to be passed down from generation to generation, yet most of the women in Genesis were initially barren. Who was *not* barren?

a. Rachel   c. Tamar
b. Sarah   d. Rebekah

17. In revealing himself to Moses and the Israelites, God said his name was:

a. Father   c. Jealous
b. Yahweh   d. The All-Merciful

18. Although Abraham is often considered the founder of monotheism, it is clear in the Pentateuch that many non-Hebrews worshipped the one, true God. Pick the person who seems *not* to have believed in God.

a. Melchizedek   c. Abimelech
b. Jethro   d. Bera

19. Who buried Moses?

a. Aaron   c. Joshua
b. God   d. The elders

WHAT AND WHY

20. Adam's excuse for eating of the tree of knowledge was:

     a. the serpent had tricked him into it
     b. the woman gave him the fruit
     c. he wanted wisdom to understand God's word
     d. he didn't know he wasn't supposed to

21. Cain murdered Abel because:

    a. he was jealous of Adam's affection for his younger brother
    b. he was jealous when God chose Abel's sacrifice over his
    c. he was envious of Abel's cattle and sheep since he had none
    d. he was lured into a rage by Abel's tauntings

22. The Lord made a covenant with Abraham in his ninety-ninth year, and as a token ordered Abraham to:

    a. sacrifice his son Ishmael
    b. give a tithe to the priest Melchizedek
    c. destroy all his household gods
    d. circumcise himself and all his men

23. The angel who was about to destroy Sodom kept hurrying Lot to flee, even taking him by the arm when he hesitated, because:

    a. otherwise Lot and his family would be killed in the conflagration
    b. he couldn't destroy the town until Lot was safe
    c. the townspeople were about to assault his daughters
    d. he was afraid Lot was about to warn the townspeople

24. God destroyed Sodom because of its rampant:

a. homosexuality　　　　c. contempt
b. greed　　　　　　　　d. inhospitality

TWO SETS OF THE TEN COMMANDMENTS

In the Orthodox and Protestant Churches the prohibition against false worship is rendered as the First and Second Commandments, but in the Catholic and Lutheran Churches it is contained in the First. The subsequent Commandments are therefore numbered differently, with the final prohibition against coveting split into two separate Commandments by Catholics and Lutherans to reach the number ten. The first version follows Origen from the second century; the second version follows Augustine from the fourth century. In the Bible itself the Commandments are not numbered.

---

25. Sarah told Abraham to cast out his concubine Hagar and her son, Ishmael, because:

　　　a. she didn't want Ishmael to share in the inheritance with her son Isaac
　　　b. she was afraid he loved Hagar more than her
　　　c. Abraham spent more time with Hagar than with Sarah
　　　d. Hagar hoarded all the best things for herself and her son

26. Soon after he arrived in Egypt and made a success of himself, Joseph was tossed into prison by his master, Potiphar, because:

    a. Potiphar's wife accused him of attempted rape
    b. Potiphar's servant accused him of theft
    c. Pharaoh discovered he was a Hebrew
    d. Pharaoh's minister heard he was interpreting dreams

27. On his way to Egypt to confront Pharaoh, Moses was nearly killed by God because:

    a. he had not circumcised his son
    b. he tarried too long, trying to avoid his mission
    c. he forgot to make a burned sacrifice
    d. he considered overthrowing Pharaoh and making himself king

28. God sent ten plagues over Egypt to break Pharaoh's stubborn will in refusing to release the Hebrews. Which of these was *not* one of the plagues?

    a. swarms of locusts   c. infestation of ants
    b. overrunning of frogs   d. swarms of flies

29. As they crossed the desert from the oasis at Elim to Mt. Sinai, the Israelites ran out of food. To quiet their complaining, the Lord provided them with:

    a. grasshoppers   c. hidden supplies
    b. bread   d. manna

30. There is only one instance in the Bible where God manifests himself on earth and does not speak. It is:

        a. when he causes the bush to burn
        b. when the seventy elders of Israel break bread on Mt. Sinai
        c. when the Israelites fashion a golden calf
        d. when Miriam rebels against Moses

31. The Ten Commandments were chiseled on stone tablets by:

a. bolts of lightning   c. the finger of God
b. angels   d. Moses

32. Which of these is *not* one of the Ten Commandments?

        a. Thou shalt love thy neighbor as thyself.
        b. Honor thy father and thy mother.
        c. Remember the Sabbath day, to keep it holy.
        d. Thou shalt not covet thy neighbor's house.

33. God commanded the Hebrews to establish three national feast days to celebrate annually. Which was *not* one of those days?

a. Passover   c. Feast of Tabernacles
b. Pentecost   d. Hanukkah

CHAPTER 3

THE HISTORICAL BOOKS

≈≈≈

The Bible, what a book! Large and wise as the
world based on the abysses of creation, and
towering aloft into the blue secrets of heaven.
Sunrise and sunset, promise and fulfillment,
birth and death—the whole drama of humanity
—are contained in this one book. It is the Book
of Books.

—HEINRICH HEINE

THE TWELVE HISTORICAL BOOKS FROM JOSHUA THROUGH ES-
ther cover approximately 1,055 years, or a period
roughly comparable in modern history from Alfred
the Great until today. They begin with the death of
Moses and the conquest of Canaan and end in the
post-Exilic period of about 400 B.C. By contrast, the
earliest Roman writings aren't known until approximately 300 B.C.

The histories are easier to follow if they are divided
into three chronological periods that are marked by
three different forms of government: the Theocracy,
during which the Hebrews were ruled by judges; the
Monarchy, when they were ruled by kings; and the
Captivity, when they were ruled by foreigners.

Joshua continues where Deuteronomy leaves off.
Having been led out of bondage by Moses and into

the Promised Land by Joshua, the Hebrew tribes now partition the territory as they move to conquer and subdue it. The conquest and resettlement must have been hugely complex, and it is represented as taking years in *Judges* and *1 Samuel*, but it is represented here as a single military mission. (In Hebrew, Joshua means "salvation" or "savior," and in the Greek is spelled *Iesous*, or Jesus.)

Judges, named after the wisdom leaders like Deborah and warriors like Gideon who became tribal governors during the period, covers the century and a half before a king arose in Israel. It takes us from the sublime heights of victory to the common and everyday failure of the people to live up to the Covenant. Seven times they fall into apostasy, seven times they are punished, seven times they repent, and seven times they are delivered. It contains the ancient "Song of Deborah" (5:2–31).

Ruth tells a story that occurred during the period of Judges and was originally attached to it. (It was separated out on a separate scroll so that it could more conveniently be publicly read at services marking Pentecost.) Ruth may be the world's first novella; nearly two-thirds of its text is dialogue. It probably derives from a true incident, in which a Moabite woman so impressed her new Hebrew relations with her constancy and fidelity that the story entered the oral tradition. The story pointedly reminds the Hebrews that Gentiles, too, can play a role in Covenant history.

1 and *2 Samuel* begin the monarchial period. The prophet Samuel is the last of the judges and anoints the first of the kings, Saul, only to watch as he psychologically disintegrates. The rise of David, Saul's attempts to kill him, and David's ascension to the throne make for compelling biography. By the time the historical account reaches the disputed succession to David's throne, it is relying on eyewitness material. The reigns of David and Solomon from 1004 to 926 B.C. are considered the golden age of the nation of Israel.

1 and 2 Kings tells of the fall of the United Kingdom after Solomon's death, the Divided Kingdoms of Judah (the southern kingdom) and Israel (the northern kingdom) which lasted approximately 270 years until Israel fell to Assyria, and the remaining Single Kingdom which is finally conquered by Babylon and exiled. The easiest way to keep these straight is to remember that Judah remained in the Davidic—and therefore Messianic—line and raised up good kings as well as bad. The northern, rebellious kingdom's rulers were uniformly bad, which resulted in continual conflicts between the two. The 130-year period of the Single Kingdom, by the way, saw the rise of the great prophets Isaiah and Jeremiah, as well as Nahum, Zephaniah, and Habakkuk.

1 and 2 Chronicles is the official ecclesiastical history of the Jewish race from Adam to the proclamation of Cyrus allowing the return to Jerusalem. It parallels the other accounts, except that it ignores the northern kingdom altogether and gives more attention to exclusively religious interpretations of the historical record. It takes great care to establish the genealogical record of the twelve tribes and especially of Judah, the Messianic line.

Ezra was almost certainly the compiler of Chronicles, and he continues the history by recounting Zerubbabel's rebuilding of the temple and his own return to Jerusalem to take charge of the spiritual stewardship of the people. There is a gap between the two accounts of about sixty years, in which the story of Esther takes place.

Nehemiah is a personal account of the Jewish governor sent to restore civil order in Jerusalem and takes place during the reign of Xerxes' son, Artaxerxes I. Ezra's efforts at reform have been stymied, the city is in disrepair, and abuses in religion and government proliferate. Nehemiah doesn't hesitate to take bold action, and his autobiography shows energy, judgment, and courage. The prophet Malachi lived at this time and denounced many of the evils Nehemiah was determined to stanch.

Esther comes before Nehemiah in time, but not in the canonical order of the Bible. It tells a story about those who did not return to Jerusalem after Babylon fell but remained behind in lands controlled by the conqueror, Persia. The king's name in Hebrew is Anasueris, in Greek *Xerxes*. The story takes place after his defeat by the Greeks at Salamis, when the historian Herodotus tells us he sought consolation in his harem. The book seems highly contrived and historically doubtful; Martin Luther called it "worthless." It is the only book of the Old Testament not found among the Dead Sea Scrolls; interestingly, it is also the only book in which God is not mentioned.

Although composed by different people in very different eras, these Histories retain a coherence and point of view that bind them into a single narrative as compelling as any history written since. Even so, they do not claim to be "history" in the sense of the discipline we know today. The Battle of Salamis, for example, one of the turning points in world history, isn't even mentioned. The great empires of Egypt, Babylon,

Assyria, and Persia, the great city-states of Phoenicia and Greece and Syria, and the great personalities who conquered nations or expanded civilization are only touched upon if they somehow affect the driving narrative point, which is the story of Redemption at work through the vessel of a Chosen People.

SELECTED READINGS:
Joshua 1–10, 20–24; Judges; Ruth; 1 Samuel 2–4, 7–11, 13–29, 31; 2 Samuel; 1 Kings 1–14, 16–19, 21–22; 2 Kings 2–10, 13, 17–25; Ezra 1, 3–7, 9–11; Nehemiah 1–3, 8, 13; Esther.

Answers begin on page 151.

MEMORABLE COMMENTS

1. When the Hebrews settled in Canaan they were unable to dislodge many of the native tribes, and in fact began to make pacts with them in disobedience of God's will. God told them these people would be:

    a. burrs under their saddles
    b. sand in their sandals
    c. thorns in their sides
    d. grist for their mills

2. After the death of her husband and two married sons, the widowed Naomi returned to Judah. Her daughter-in-law, a Moabite and also a widow, insisted on going with her, saying:

a. Two heads are better than one.
b. Life without thee is a curse.
c. Whither thou goest, I will go.
d. Parting is such sweet sorrow.

3. When the tribes of Israel gathered, Samuel, acting at God's command, picked from the tribe of Benjamin a man named Saul to be the new king, and the people responded:

a. God save the king.
b. Behold the man
c. Better late than never.
d. We are in God's hand.

4. When Saul delayed an attack on the Philistines and offered a burnt sacrifice himself instead of waiting for Samuel to do it, Samuel reproved him, saying the Lord sought:

a. an honest man
b. peace in our time
c. a man after his own heart
d. to put him through his paces

5. David led a rebellion against Saul and even joined the Philistines in opposing him. When the news reached David that Saul and his heir Jonathan had been killed in battle, he exclaimed:

a. Will wonders never cease?
b. Fortune favors the brave.
c. How are the mighty fallen!
d. They were good men and true.

NOW, A WORD ON THE WORD

The word *bible* comes from the Greek *biblion*, or book, and its plural *biblia*. The Bible is, in effect, The Books. The Greek word, in turn, derives from *byblos*, or papyrus, and comes from the name of the Phoenician seaport Byblos, which produced and exported papyrus for writing throughout the ancient world. By the fifth century A.D. it became the common term for all the Scriptures, ancient and Christian. A layman, Tertullian of Carthage, first used the term *Novum Testamentum* to distinguish the Gospels and Apostic Writings from the Hebrew canon, in circa A.D. 200.

6. When Hezekiah, king of Judah, was dying, the prophet Isaiah came to him and said he should:

a. set his house in order
b. say his prayers
c. repent, for the end is near
d. fight to the last gasp

FAMOUS PEOPLE

7. Spies sent into Jericho by Joshua were discovered, but escaped when they were hidden by:

a. the princess Hadassah   c. the harlot Rahab
b. the prophetess Deborah   d. the innkeeper Vashti

8. The Canaanites sent their war captain Sisera to drive the Hebrews back. As his army was being defeated, he fled on foot, finally reaching the tent of Jael, wife of Heber, who:

    a. pulled him inside, then lied to the pursuing Hebrews

    b. burned down her tent to prevent him from hiding

    c. lulled him to sleep, then drove a nail through his temple

    d. comforted him at her bosom and ran away with him

9. When Gideon tore down the altar of Baal, he was frightened by the ferocity of the Gentiles' anger against him, and to make sure he really was chosen by God for his mission he devised the test of:

    a. the lion and the rope

    b. the fleece and the dew

    c. the calf and the milk

    d. the rainbow and the dawn

10. Jephthah, called to defeat the Ammonites, gave a vow to the Lord that if he won he would:

    a. sacrifice whatever first came out of his house to greet him

    b. destroy all the temples of the heathen

    c. shave his head and dedicate his life to the Lord

    d. slaughter a hundred cattle and three hundred sheep for a feast

11. An angel of the Lord appeared to Samson's mother and told her:

    a. Behold . . . thou shalt conceive and bear a son.
    b. You will raise up a mighty man of valor.
    c. You will weep and gnash your teeth.
    d. Flee, for the wrath of the Lord be upon you.

12. Naomi told Ruth to make her desire for Boaz known to him by:

    a. lifting her veil in his presence
    b. lying at his feet while he slept
    c. following him while he reaped his corn
    d. weaving for him a coat of many colors

13. Before David came to the attention of the royal court he was known as a:

    a. harpist
    b. potential rival
    c. disciple of Samuel
    d. composer of psalms

14. When news reached David of Saul's death, he promptly:

    a. moved to take over the army
    b. declared thirty days of rejoicing
    c. killed the messenger
    d. donned sackcloth and ashes

15. David brought the ark of the Covenant into Jerusalem, leaping and dancing before it clad only in a linen vestment, while his wife, Michal, looked through a window:

a. adored him   c. cheered him
b. despised him   d. called out to him

16. David was nearly forced from his throne by the rebellion of his son:

a. Amnon   c. Solomon
b. Absolom   d. Abonijeh

17. When God appeared to Solomon in a dream and said, "Ask what shall I give thee," Solomon asked for:

a. a long life   c. riches beyond
                          compare
b. death to mine   d. an understanding
   enemies   heart

18. The wicked king Ahab was utterly seduced into following the gods of his wife:

a. Jezebel   c. Sapphira
b. Ishtar   d. Salome I

WHAT AND WHY

19. Before the Hebrews launched their campaign against Jericho, God ordered Joshua to:

a. offer a burnt offering   c. recruit trumpeters
b. circumcise his men   d. prepare siege towers

20. The Hebrew tribes, except for Judah, had a hard time dislodging the inhabitants of Canaan because:

a. they quarreled too much among themselves
b. the inhabitants had chariots of iron
c. they whored after the gods of the Moabites
d. Joshua's death left them without a general

21. Deborah, the prophetess, judged Israel from her place:

a. by the Jordan
b. by the walls of Shiloh
c. under a palm tree
d. before the tabernacle

22. Jotham was the only son of Gideon not to be murdered by his brother Abimelech, and Jotham prophesied against Abimelech with the parable of:

a. the trees who wanted a king
b. the fox who ate sour grapes
c. the tortoise and the rabbit
d. the boy who cried wolf

23. Samson made a wager with the guests at his engagement feast over:

a. who was strongest   c. a riddle
b. who had the longest   d. a race
   hair

24. When the traveling Levite found that his concubine had been raped and murdered by the men of Gibeah, he:

a. vowed to burn the city to the ground
b. cut her body into pieces
c. mourned her for forty days
d. killed himself

WHO CUT OFF SAMSON'S HAIR?

Hint: It wasn't Delilah. See Judges 16:19.

---

25. When the Lord first called the prophet Samuel, the young boy thought:

a. it was the voice of his master Eli
b. it was the voice of an evil spirit
c. he was dreaming
d. he was doomed

26. When Saul feared for the worst before his final battle with the Philistines, he secretly visited a woman who had:

a. a plan of escape   c. a way with runes
b. a familiar spirit   d. a sacrificial lamb

27. David united the kingdoms of Judah and Israel and placed the new capital at:

a. Jerusalem   c. Sechem
b. Hebron   d. Shiloh

28. David had Uriah the Hittite sent to the front lines, where he was killed in battle, and then married Bathsheba because:

a. she was pregnant
b. he had seen her washing herself
c. he needed an heir
d. it fulfilled a prophecy

29. When his older brother Adonijah asked permission to marry, Solomon responded by:

a. kissing him on both cheeks
b. slapping him across the face
c. telling a famous proverb
d. putting him to death

30. The Queen of Sheba made a state visit to Jerusalem to meet Solomon because she wanted to:

a. make an alliance

b. marry him

c. ask him hard questions

d. sit at his feet

31. Elijah the prophet killed the messengers of the Israelite king to keep them from reaching Beelzebub, who was:

a. the god of Ekron

b. the priestess of Sheol

c. the warlock of Gezeb

d. the prince of Gehenna

32. When Elijah fled to a cave to escape the king's wrath, the Lord came to him as:

a. a great and strong wind

b. fire

c. a still small voice

d. an earthquake

33. God's punishment, so long foretold, came true when the Assyrians captured and caused to vanish from history forever the tribes of:

a. Israel   c. Edom

b. Moab   d. Canaan

34. When Sargon's son Sennacherib besieged Jerusalem, the city was saved when:

    a. his army was struck by a plague

    b. mice gnawed on and broke his army's bowstrings

    c. lightning struck the enemy headquarters

    d. an angel killed most of the attackers

35. Josia, the seventeenth king of Judah in the Davidic line, ordered the restoration of the Temple. During the interior reconstruction the high priest discovered:

    a. the book of the Law

    b. the treasure of Solomon

    c. the well of the Jesubites

    d. the ark of the Covenant

36. Jerusalem and the Temple were finally destroyed by:

a. Nebuchadnezzer   c. Sargon III

b. Hammurabi   d. Ataxerxes

37. The rebuilding of the Temple under Cyrus and his son, Darius, was opposed by:

a. Israelites
b. Samaritans

c. Babylonians
d. Assyrians

38. After the Temple was rebuilt, the scribe Ezra read aloud:

    a. the decree of Cyrus allowing the Jews to return
    b. the book of the Law of Moses
    c. the decree of exile for all foreigners
    d. the psalm of David on the ark of the Covenant

CHAPTER 4

THE WISDOM BOOKS

≈≈≈

The greater the intellectual progress of the
ages, the more fully it will be possible to employ the Bible not only as the Foundation, but
as the instrument of education.

—JOHANN WOLFGANG VON GOETHE

THE WISDOM LITERATURE OF THE OLD TESTAMENT MAKES
the Bible more than a book of law or a history of the
Covenant: its lessons are now leavened with poetry.
These books display every emotion we encounter in
religion and in life: abandonment, hope, joy, disillu-
sionment, anger, grief, confusion, resignation, yearn-
ing, and gratitude.

When Jeremiah wrote that "the law shall not depart
from the priest, nor counsel from the wise, nor the
word from the prophet" (Jer 18:18), he neatly summa-
rized the themes to be found in the Old Testament.
The priests give the law and write the histories. The
prophets pronounce the word and preach its fulfillment. The philosophers give counsel. The Wisdom literature belongs to the philosophers; now narrative
gives way to poetry.

CAPITAL CITIES IN THE OLD TESTAMENT

Babylon: Capital city of Mesopotamian and Chaldean empires (c. 2000 to 539 B.C.) and the place of exile for the Judean captivity, located on the Euphrates River in modern Iraq.

Damascus: Capital of Syria and the oldest continually occupied city in the world (Gen 14:16).

Hebron: Abraham's home after his return from Egypt (Gen 13) and David's capital when he ruled Judah (2 Sam 2:1–4).

Jerusalem: Stronghold of the Jesubites captured by David and made into the capital of the United Kingdom of Judah and Israel (2 Sam 5:6–7).

Ninevah: Capital of the Assyrian empire (c. 700 to 612 B.C.), located on the Tigris River in modern Iraq. (See the Book of Nahum.)

Samaria: Capital city of the Northern Kingdom of Israel, built by Omri in 880 B.C. (1 Kgs 16:23–24).

Shechem: Site of Rehoboam's crowning as king of Israel after Solomon's death (1 Kgs 12:1) and first capital of the Northern Kingdom.

Shiloh: Religious capital of the Hebrews and site of the ark of the Covenant before David moved it to Jerusalem, located twenty miles south of Jerusalem.

Ur: Capital of the ancient Sumerian empire (c. 2600 to 2100 B.C.) and important trading center until the fourth century B.C. Early home of Abraham (Gen 11:31), located on the Euphrates in modern Iraq.

Wisdom literature flourished throughout the Fertile Crescent, and writings have survived from Egypt, Mesopotamia, and Greece. Old stories, myths, aphorisms, bits of poetry, fables, and wise sayings crossed

THE WISDOM BOOKS ≈ 53

and recrossed national and tribal boundaries. Indeed, in poetic structure and form, many Egyptian texts are very close to the Hebrew Wisdom literature, and in some cases probably much older. But the Hebrew has one quality that distinguishes it from all the literature of its time: it is God-centered and God-seeking. As Proverbs 1:7 puts it, "The fear of the Lord is the beginning of knowledge." The search for understanding God's will and following his dictates permeates the Wisdom literature and endows it with a unique character and insight.

Job is a good example. The story of Job is certainly very old, which is why the book once was thought to be the oldest in the Bible, dating from the time of the Patriarchs or before. The Job counterpart can be found in many ancient legends, and the name is found in non-Hebrew documents of the eighteenth century B.C. This fits with the Biblical account, for Job is seen as a pre-Hebrew Semitic. The "patience of Job" was as legendary in ancient times as it is today, but this does not square with the impatient central character of the book as we have it. The Hebrew writer has taken this ancient story of the suffering but faithful Job as his starting point. Into it he has inserted his own deep poetic reflections on man's problematic relationship with God, giving voice through the various characters to traditional explanations of evil, but finally casting all these aside to declare that God's wisdom is beyond man's comprehension and that love of God is an end into itself.

The story of Job as presented in the Old Testament canon is one of the great classics of Western civilization. Thomas Carlyle said it was "one of the grandest things ever written." I recommend that the reader encounter the book first in a newer translation, and then read the King James Version to gain the full benefit of its grandeur. Don't be surprised if Job's friends seem reasonable—they are, after all, making all the arguments that reason and conventional piety have come up with. And don't be bewildered if God's response to Job seems disconcerting; God has no intention of answering the question posed. He refuses to be cast as a kind of cosmic scorekeeper. It is his very majesty that illuminates the emptiness of man's attempts to describe him.

Psalms is a collection of five separate anthologies of 150 sacred songs composed over a period of five hundred years—or roughly the period in English poetry from Chaucer to Yeats. For all this distance in time from the first to the last, the Psalms are remarkably—amazingly—consistent in style, form, and idiom. In almost every other case in the Bible, the revelation is of God's word to man. In the Psalms we have man's word to God. The principal kinds of Psalms which can be distinguished by their subject are: psalms of thanksgiving, praise, and worship; prayers of penitence, entreaty, and vengeance; oracles of prophecy; and songs to the king. (After the fall of the monarchy, the royal songs—addressed as they are to the descendents of David—were often reinterpreted in a messianic light and quoted along with the prophetic Psalms.)

Jesus quotes the Psalms directly twelve times, including three times during his passion on the cross. In his last words before his Ascension he said: "All things must be fulfilled which were written in the law of Moses, and in the prophets, and in the Psalms concerning me" (Luke 24:44).

Proverbs is a practical book that combines the best of Solomon's sayings (out of the 3,000 he is said to have written) with other wise teachings as an instruction for the young. To the question of why one should follow the commandments, *Leviticus* might answer, "Because it's the Law." The prophets might answer, "Because it's God's will." *Proverbs* answers, "Because it's the prudent thing to do." Its main message is order and discipline; to its authors, the highest attribute is self-control. Despite the fact that the human mind cannot begin to comprehend the ways of God, a man can and should take care to comprehend the ways of the world.

Ecclesiastes (or "The Preacher" from the Greek *ekklesia*, church, and Latin *ecclesiastes*, speaker) has been called the sphinx of Hebrew literature. Its language and style do not correspond to any writings known from any stage of Hebrew history. Its skepticism and world-weariness contrast sharply with the positive instructional tone of *Proverbs*, which is probably why it is placed immediately after, like ballast on a ship. Its main theme is the utter emptiness of human existence and the futility of attempting anything in a world where good and evil, wisdom and folly, are rewarded with the same end: "And how dieth the wise man? As the fool" (Eccl 2:16). After surveying his life and noting the inconsequentiality of riches and power and knowledge—all man's vaunted attainments—the Preacher concludes that nothing is left but to "serve God and keep his commandments: this is the whole duty of man."

The Song of Songs is a series of love poems in which

the two lovers are united, then separated, sought, then found. Recent attempts to read it literally as a testimonial to married love are as wrongheaded as past attempts to explain it away with elaborate and sometimes farfetched symbolic interpretations. Rather, the Song should be seen as a controlling metaphor for all of Scripture, expressing the intense and even passionate love of the Creator for his creation in terms as intense and passionate as humans can get. The convenantal relationship is expressed erotically as a love affair, with all the hopes and disappointments, joys and pleasures, misunderstandings and reconciliations that love affairs bring and which characterized the relationship between God and Israel. Certainly this was the allegorical understanding that led the great sage Rabbi Akiva to pronounce it divinely inspired (calling it "the Holy of Holies") and which led it to be included in the Hebrew canon at the council of Jamnia in A.D. 90. The same understanding led St. Bernard of Clairvaux, a doctor of the Church, to call it "the heart of the mystical life."

The Song is composed along the lines of a semidramatic wedding song, with the king, his bride, and a chorus. It seems to have been a Near Eastern custom to present such idylls, complete with music and dance, at the wedding ceremony, perhaps with the bride and groom playing the roles of king and queen. This would be the natural form to use in a mystical reverie that celebrates God's marriage—his covenant —with his chosen people, making it indeed the song of all songs.

These five books of Wisdom literature, especially as interpreted in the King James Version, are entrenched in the Western literary consciousness. Regardless of one's religion—or lack of it—they are the foundations of education and culture; no individual can aspire to either without a thorough familiarity with their language or knowledge of their contents. They are so dense with emotion and rich in complexity that only by reading them over and over again can the reader penetrate all the layers of meaning they contain or comprehend the sublimity of the message they offer in so many different and deeper ways.

SELECTED READINGS:
Job; Psalms 1, 2, 4, 6, 8, 9, 14–16, 19–24, 27, 29, 30, 37, 39, 42, 43, 45–49, 51, 62, 63, 65, 67, 68, 72, 84, 85, 87–93, 95, 97, 100–4, 107, 110, 114–16, 120–31, 133, 136, 137, 139, 145, 147–50; Proverbs 1, 4–23, 25–31; Ecclesiastes; Song of Songs.

Answers begin on page 170.

MEMORABLE COMMENTS

1. Job mourned that "Man that is born of woman is of few days, and full of trouble," and he eventually would:

    a. go the way of all flesh
    b. eat his heart out
    c. give up the ghost
    d. sleep through an ever-enduring night

2. In the midst of his afflictions, Job begs his friend Bildad to have pity on him, recounting his afflictions and saying he:

    a. has made it by the seat of his pants
    b. has escaped by the skin of his teeth
    c. would survive by hook or by crook
    d. had come within an inch of his life

3. Even though he suffered greatly and complained bitterly, Job never relented in his faith because, he said:

    a. I know that my redeemer liveth.
    b. While I breathe I hope.
    c. Pain is short but joy is eternal.
    d. We are in God's hands.

4. When God confronted Job from "out of the whirlwind," he told him to:

    a. gird up his loins like a man
    b. prepare to die like a dog
    c. crawl on his belly like a serpent
    d. eat the dust like a worm

5. David extols God's greatness, saying he has perfected praise:

    a. from sea to shining sea
    b. out of the mouth of babes
    c. from the four corners of the earth
    d. out of dust and spit

6. David asked the Lord to look upon him as:

    a. the apple of his eye
    b. the jewel in his crown
    c. the flower of his garden
    d. the shepherd of his flock

7. In his seven last words on the cross, Jesus quotes Psalms twice. Which is one of those quotes?

> a. Father, forgive them; for they know not what they do.
> b. Father, into thy hands I commend my spirit.
> c. Today thou shalt be with me in paradise.
> d. Woman, behold thy son.

8. According to Psalm 37, the righteous should not be dismayed over the apparent prosperity of evildoers because:

> a. the meek shall inherit the earth
> b. justice triumphs over all
> c. all's well that ends well
> d. the wheel will come full circle

9. Psalm 55 is the strongest statement in the Bible about the cruelty of false friendship. The Psalmist bemoans the friend who betrayed him, saying:

> a. The evil that men do lives after them.
> b. He flew under false colors.
> c. His words were smooth as butter.
> d. There shall be no love lost.

10. Proverbs cautions not to follow folly but enter the house built on:

> a. the seven pillars of wisdom
> b. a foundation of rock
> c. prayer
> d. great deeds

11. Ecclesiastes is jaded about almost everything he sees, concluding that:

       a. Beauty is only skin deep.
       b. Beauty is in the eye of the beholder.
       c. There is nothing new under the sun.
       d. Here today, gone tomorrow.

12. In his typically world-weary way, Ecclesiastes notes that:

       a. The race never ends.
       b. The race goes not to the swift.
       c. He wins the race who runs by himself.
       d. Slow and steady wins the race.

THE PSALMISTS' FAMOUS PHRASES

13. "Why do the heathen rage, and imagine . . ."

    a. our destruction   c. a victory
    b. a vain thing   d. the hills will
                               answer

ANSWER NOT A FOOL ACCORDING TO HIS FOLLY. MAYBE.

According to Proverbs 6:5: "Answer not a fool according to his folly, lest thou also be like unto him." But hold it. The very next verse says: "Answer a fool according to his folly, lest he be wise in his own conceit."

14. "For thou hast made him a little lower than . . ."

    a. the gods   c. the angels
    b. the mountain tops d. the giants of the
                                earth

15. "He rode upon a cherub and did fly: yea, he did fly upon . . ."

    a. the wings of eagles
    b. the wings of the wind
    c. the wings of angels
    d. the wings of righteousness

16. "The heavens declare the glory of God; and the firmament showeth . . ."

    a. his splendor   c. his fearfulness
    b. his radiance   d. his handiwork

17. "The earth is the Lord's, and the fullness thereof, the world, and . . ."

    a. the waters that flow upon it
    b. they that dwell within
    c. all abounding on it
    d. the heavens above

18. "Sing unto him . . ."

    a. with instruments and strings
    b. a new song
    c. the glory of his world
    d. thanksgiving

19. "Be still, and know . . ."

    a. that all is well
    b. the quiet that refresheth the soul
    c. that I am God
    d. the indwelling of my spirit

20. "We spend our years as . . ."

    a. best we can
    b. children playing in a field
    c. lightly as the air
    d. a tale that is told

LITERARY FORMS IN THE BIBLE

Ode. Poem meant to be sung (from the Greek *aude,* voice). Many of the psalms contain instructions on the music to which they are to be set. These range from processionals such as Psalm 68, to anthems such as 105, to simple songs such as 13 and 14.

Lyric. The writer expresses his feelings and emotions, which can range from the reflective to the rhapsodical, as seen in Psalm 23 and 100, respectively.

Elegy. Lamentation, as with Psalm 137.

Epic. "The story of a people when it decides to become a people," according to author Louise Cowan. No better example than Exodus.

Drama. Poetic dialogue, as in the Book of Job.

Idyllic. The poetic description of a scene or series of scenes that is picturesque, as in the Song of Songs.

21. "The days of our years are . . ."

    a. threescore and ten
    b. fourscore and seven
    c. brief as a candle's flicker
    d. weighed with care

22. "So teach us to . . ."

    a. know thy strength
    b. count our blessings
    c. forsake the evildoer
    d. number our days

23. "I said in my haste, . . ."

    a. all men are liars   c. all or nothing
    b. all is vanity   d. there is no God

24. "Precious in the sight of the Lord is . . ."

    a. the tabernacle and all within
    b. the worship of his people
    c. the birth of his beloved ones
    d. the death of his saints

25. "The stone which the builders refused is become the . . ."

    a. cornerstone
    b. new foundation
    c. instrument of their deaths
    d. obstacle to salvation

26. "Blessed be he that cometh . . ."

    a. singing thy praises
    b. in truth and wisdom
    c. in the name of the Lord
    d. to aid the afflicted

27. "Thy word is a lamp unto my feet, and . . ."

    a. a light unto my path
    b. a beacon for the just
    c. a balefire to the wicked
    d. a flame to the pure of heart

28. "I will lift up mine eyes unto the hills, from whence cometh my . . ."

    a. salvation   c. strength
    b. Lord   d. help

29. "I was glad when they said unto me, Let us go . . ."

    a. into the house of the Lord
    b. to the valley of Hebron
    c. beside the still waters
    d. onto the highest mountain

30. "They that sow in tears shall reap in . . ."

    a. sorrow   c. glory
    b. joy   d. bitterness

31. "Except the Lord build the house, they labor in vain that build it; except the Lord keep the city . . ."

a. the watchman waketh but in vain
b. the walls shall tremble and fall down
c. they that dwelleth therein shall not sleep
d. the lamps shall flicker and go out

32. "By the rivers of Babylon, there we sat down, yea, we wept, when we remembered . . ."

a. Jerusalem   c. Israel
b. Judah   d. Zion

33. "I will fear thee: for I am . . ."

a. alight with the instance of thy glory
b. thy good servant
c. fearfully and wonderfully made
d. standing in the stead of the angels

34. "Put not your trust in . . ."

a. your fellow men   c. the things of this world
b. Satan   d. princes

35. "Let every thing that hath breath . . ."

a. cry out to thee   c. live by your law
b. see your glory   d. praise the Lord

THE PSALM OF THE CROSS

36. Psalm 22 begins with the great lamentation "My God, my God, why hast thou forsaken me?"—which Jesus uttered in his passion. Which of these actions

while Jesus suffered on the cross is *not* prophesied in
this psalm?

> a. the piercing of his hands and feet
> b. the casting of lots for his robe
> c. the darkness over the land
> d. the taunting of the passersby

THE TWENTY-THIRD PSALM

37. Test your knowledge of this great poem by filling in the blanks:

> The Lord is my _____; I shall not
> _____.
> He maketh me to lie down _____
> _____: he leadeth me beside the
> _____. He _____ my soul: he
> leadeth me in the _____ of righteousness for
> _____ sake. Yea, though I walk through
> the _____ I will fear _____: for
> thou art with me; thy _____ they
> comfort me. Thou preparest a _____ before me in
> the presence of _____: thou an-
> nointest my head with _____; my _____ run-
> neth over.
> Surely _____ and _____ shall
> follow me all the days of my life: and I will dwell
> _____ for ever.

PROVERBIAL STATEMENTS

38. "Wisdom is the principal thing; therefore get wisdom: and with all thy getting get . . ."

a. a good wife   c. understanding
b. wealth   d. education

39. "The lips of a strange woman drop as a honeycomb, and her mouth is . . ."

a. deceitful as the viper
b. smoother than oil
c. roguish with tempting words
d. sweeter than wine

40. "Go to the ant, thou sluggard; consider her ways, and . . ."

a. be wise   c. awaken
b. work hard   d. store away for
                         winter months

41. "Can a man take fire in his bosom, and his . . . ?"

a. lesson not be learned
b. heart not be set aflame
c. clothes not be burned
d. skin not be scorched

SPEAK FOR YOURSELF, SOLOMON

Solomon is traditionally regarded as the original author of most of the proverbs, including 18:22: "Whoso find a wife findeth a good thing . . ." Solomon certainly followed his own advice. According to 1 Kings 11:3, he had 700 wives and 300 concubines.

42. "With her much fair speech she caused him to yield, with the flattering of her lips she forced him. He goeth after her straightway, . . ."

    a. like a duckling after its mother
    b. as a bull chargest the cape
    c. like a flag followeth the breeze
    d. as an ox goeth to the slaughter

43. "Stolen waters are sweet, and bread eaten in secret is . . ."

    a. pleasant   c. crusty
    b. stale   d. unwholesome

44. "In the multitude of counsellors there is . . ."

    a. confusion   c. discord
    b. inspiration   d. safety

45. "As a jewel of gold in a swine's snout, so is a fair woman which is . . ."

    a. not yet married   c. unloved by her
                         husband
    b. without discretion d. also with riches

46. "He that troubleth his own house shall . . ."

    a. cause the roofbeam to fall
    b. set his children's teeth on edge
    c. inherit the wind
    d. receive no inheritance

47. "Hope deferred maketh . . ."

    a. dirt into dust   c. the temples throb
    b. the heart sick   d. grown men weep

48. "Desire accomplished is . . ."

    a. sweet to the soul
    b. dangerous to behold
    c. a snare for the unwitting
    d. a prelude to peace

49. "He that spareth his rod . . ."

    a. receiveth his reward
    b. spoileth the child
    c. loveth evil
    d. hateth his son

50. "A soft answer turneth away . . ."

    a. friends   c. wrath
    b. the merchant   d. sorrow

51. "Pride goeth before . . ."

    a. haughtiness   c. a fall
    b. destruction   d. honor

52. "Wealth maketh many . . ."

a. sorrows   c. friends

b. troubles   d. tempters

53. "Train up a child in the way he should go; and when he is old, he will . . ."

    a. be ungrateful

    b. not depart from it

    c. regret hard words

    d. straighten his path

54. "Seest thou a man diligent in his business? He shall . . ."

    a. heap up mountains of gold

    b. rise up early

    c. never be cheated

    d. stand before kings

55. "Put a knife to thy throat, if thou be a man given to . . ."

a. talebearing   c. ingratitude

b. appetite   d. lust

56. "If thine enemy be hungry . . ."

    a. give him bread to eat

    b. serve him a bowl of dust

    c. throw him the scraps from thy table

    d. let his wrongdoing feed him

57. "Answer a fool according to his . . ."

   a. deserts   c. actions
   b. welfare   d. folly

58. "Open rebuke is better than . . ."

   a. silent hate   c. wrathful looks
   b. secret love   d. pouty lips

59. "Where there is no vision . . ."

   a. no man seeth   c. the darkness
                          lingereth
   b. the people perish d. there is no good

60. "Such is the way of an adulterous woman; she
eateth, and wipeth her mouth, and saith . . ."

   a. I have done no   c. Forgive me, Father,
      wickedness.   for I have sinned.
   b. naught of her acts. d. Stolen waters are
                             sweet.

61. "Who can find a virtuous woman? for her price
is far above . . ."

   a. pearls   c. frankincense
   b. rubies   d. myrrh

SING ALONG WITH THE SONG OF SONGS

62. "Let him kiss me with the kisses of his mouth:
for thy love is better than . . ."

a. sweetness   c. wine
b. apricots   d. beauty

63. "I am the rose of Sharon, and . . ."

a. the apple of thy delight
b. the lily of the valley
c. the thistle of the high way
d. the palm that giveth shade

64. "Set me as a seal upon thy . . ."

a. people   c. household
b. country   d. heart

65. "Many waters cannot quench . . ."

a. love   c. passion
b. fire   d. embers

FAMOUS PEOPLE

66. Job makes it a point to answer every objection raised by his friends. But perhaps because he's reached the end of his famous patience, he completely ignores:

a. Eliphaz   c. Zophar
b. Elihu   d. Bildad

67. After Job repents, God turns to his friends and tells them to:

    a. pat themselves on the back
    b. don sackcloth and ashes
    c. hold a great feast of thanksgiving
    d. offer a burnt sacrifice

68. The dedication to Psalm 34 reads, "A Psalm of David, when he changed his behavior before Abimelech." David changed his behavior by:

    a. playing the coward
    b. feigning madness
    c. acting the traitor
    d. pretending blindness

69. Psalm 110 says that the Messiah will not come from the Levitical line but will be a priest according to the order of:

    a. Aaron   c. Melchizedek
    b. Joshua   d. Methuselah

CHAPTER 5

THE PROPHETS

≈≈≈

How many ages and generations have brooded and wept and agonized over this book! What untellable joys and ecstasies, what support to martyrs at the stake, from it! To what myriads has it been the shore and rock of safety—the refuge from driving tempest and wreck! Translated in all languages, how it has united this diverse world! Of its thousands there is not a verse, not a word, but is thick-studded with human emotion.

—WALT WHITMAN

THE ENTIRE OLD TESTAMENT IS A PROPHECY OF SORTS—A biography, one might say, awaiting its subject. Nowhere is that subject more sorely missed and more keenly anticipated than in the Prophetic books.

The Old Testament is full of prophets. Their names are a survey of Old Testament history, from Abraham, Moses and Deborah to Samuel, Elijah and Elisha. These are known collectively as the Former Prophets, and their prophetic work was mostly oral: We encounter them through the historical accounts.

Then the Latter Prophets take their place in the Biblical pageant, and we encounter them directly through their inspired writings. If you have your image of an Old Testament prophet firmly in mind—flowing white beard, flashing eyes, finger pointed heavenward in admonition—you might be surprised at the variety of characters God chooses as his messengers. They range from herdsmen in tattered clothes to aristocrats and even princes of Judah. They are, in fact, alike only in one thing: They have received a call and answered, "Here am I; send me."

The prophetic vision operates on three levels simultaneously. Maybe it's better to say that it *sees* ahead without regard to distance: foreground, middleground, and background are merged while remaining distinct. A prophecy, therefore, can be at once accurate for the next day, the next generation, and all time. It can be a lesson for the king to whom it was delivered, to the nation to which it was written, and to the individual reading it in the Bible today. It can be fulfilled a few passages later, as with Isaiah's famous prophecy of the coming birth of his own son, Immanuel; a few hundred years later, as it was with the Incarnation; and a few thousand years later, as it will be with the next person who accepts the Messiah —"God-with-us"—into his own heart.

A prophecy is rarely a prediction. Usually it is a moral thunderbolt hurled at a nation corrupted by greed, uncaring of the poor, and unfaithful in worship. This is what separates the Hebrew prophets from the Near Eastern seers and magicians of the surrounding nations. The prophets had both *insight* and *foresight*, but as W. Graham Scroggie pointed out, it was their insight that gave them their foresight. If they accurately foretold the fall of Israel, which they did, or the destruction of the Temple, which they did, or the captivity of Judah, which they did, it was because they could see the consequence of indifference to God. If they foretold a future Redeemer, his sacrifice, and his final glory, all of which they did, it was because they plumbed the depths of God's love for his people and foresaw salvation.

As presented in the Hebrew, Catholic, and Protestant canons of the Old Testament, the prophets appear out of chronological order, an arrangement that confuses the casual reader no end. It is best to remember that these are writings that mostly appeared during the period of 2 Kings. Isaiah, Jeremiah, Ezekial, and Daniel are presented first because of the length of their writings and their importance, and the twelve remaining (the "minor prophets") follow according to no particular scheme, except that the three post-Exilic prophets (Haggai, Zechariah, and Malachi) properly come at the end. The Hebrew canon places Lamentations and Daniel in the Writings, not among the prophets, and this has raised questions as to authenticity. The Protestant canon agrees with the Catholic as to the prophetic stature of those two books, but eliminates several others such as Baruch. (We will follow the Protestant canon.)

Isaiah is a miniature Bible. It has sixty-six chapters just as the Protestant Bible has sixty-six books. It divides so completely in emphasis and style that most scholars believe it was written by two people, Isaiah and the so-called Second Isaiah. The "first book" consists of thirty-nine chapters, just as the Old Testament contains thirty-nine books. The "second book" contains twenty-seven chapters, just as the New Testament contains twenty-seven books. The first book opens with the judgment of Judah just as the Old Testament opens with the judgment of Adam. The second book opens with "the voice of him that crieth in the wilderness" (Isa 40) just as the New Testament begins with John the Baptist (Mark 1).

Isaiah evidently saw no contradiction between his aristocratic birth and his prophetic calling. He could enter the role of the wise statesman on the one hand, and the evangelical reformer on the other, but always both to the same end. When it seemed to him that the moral regeneration of the nation was impossible, he looked to the survival of a "saving remnant" to keep the faith alive. He was given the gift of Messianic vision and was the first to proclaim his coming. Chapters 40–55 are a later addition to the book by an anonymous prophet of the Exile known as Second Isaiah. His writing is characterized by a lyric rapture and a deep understanding of the meaning and role of the Messiah as the "suffering servant" who would redeem not just Israel but the whole world.

Jeremiah was essentially a peace-loving man whose role it was to prophesize doom and destruction, so much so that a "Jeremiad" has come down in the language as a synonym for a harangue predicting woe. In Jeremiah's case, his prophecy came true with the fall of Jerusalem to Babylon.

Lamentations is traditionally attributed to Jeremiah because of its subject, the fall of Jerusalem. It is an elaborate dirge (in Hebrew it is constructed as an acrostic) that conveys the mournful emotions of the defeated nation.

Ezekiel was a priest and his devotion to ceremony has led him to be called the father of Judaism. But he was also a visionary. Of the three great prophets,

Isaiah was primarily a poet, Jeremiah the preacher, and Ezekiel the mystic. His visions make him the source of the apocalyptic tradition.

Daniel has been called "the prophet of dreams" who rose from the position of captive to be prime minister of Babylon. His calling was to display the power and might of the Hebrew God to the Gentile rulers, demonstrating to all that this was no mere local deity but the one true God of the universe. In the alternative dating, the book is meant to sustain faith among the Jews during the persecution of Antiochus Epiphanes.

The *Minor Prophets* are treated as a single book in the Hebrew Bible:

Hosea teaches that God's love is constant and stubborn despite the unfaithfulness of his people.

Joel sees a disastrous plague of locusts with the triple vision of the prophet: it is actual, allegorical, and apocalyptic. He is the first to predict the outpouring of the Holy Spirit.

Amos was a shepherd and by the dating of some scholars, the first of the Latter Prophets. He denounced social injustice and preached that a "day of the Lord" was coming as a visitation of wrath.

Obadiah denounces the Edomites for their participation in the destruction of Jerusalem and pronounces judgment on them.

Jonah shows that God's message of salvation is for all peoples, even the Assyrians of Ninevah. It also teaches obedience to God's call. In the alternative dating, it is seen as a parable teaching tolerance and the universality of God's message against the narrow tribal laws of the early post-Exilic period.

Micah foresees the ruin of Judah because of its corruption in morals and religion.

Nahum prophesizes the destruction of Ninevah with great poetic power.

Habakkuk is a poetic dialogue that reveals why God has chosen the Babylonians as the instruments for his judgment.

Zephaniah preaches a "day of retribution" and teaches that sin is not the violation of a rule or law but an offense against God.

Haggai and *Zechariah* (1–8) urge the rebuilding of the Temple and restoration of the nation. The remainder of *Zechariah* contains oracles that foresee the coming of the Messiah and the last days.

Malachi is not the name of a prophet but the Hebrew word for "my messenger." Its author is unknown. This last great prophetic seer looks forward to the "day of the Lord" which will be preceded by the return of Elijah.

With the writing of Malachi, the tradition of the prophets ends. It will be four hundred years before John the Baptist restores it as a new Elijah, "a voice crying in the wilderness."

SELECTED READINGS:

Isaiah 1–6, 9–11, 13–19, 21, 23–28, 31–32, 34–35, 38, 40, 44–45, 47, 49, 51 55, 60–63; Jeremiah 1–2, 4, 6–8, 10, 12–14, 17–20, 24–26, 29–31, 36–40, 42–44, 51; Lamentations; Ezekiel 1–5, 16–18, 23, 27, 32, 34, 37–40; Daniel; Hosea 1–3, 11, 14; Joel 1–2; Amos; Obadiah; Jonah; Micah 1, 3–6; Nahum 2–3; Habakkuk 1–2; Zephaniah 1–2; Malachi 3–4.

Answers begin on page 181.

The Prophets in Order of Appearance

The chronological order of the books or at least the appearance of the prophets themselves may have been as follows, although the books of Joel, Jonah, and Daniel are debatable by several centuries. The kingdom is the country to which the prophecies were addressed.

Prophet	Relevant History	Date (B.C.)	Kingdom
Joel	2 Kgs 11–12	837–800*	Judah
Jonah	2 Kgs 13–14	825–782*	Assyria
Amos	2 Kgs 14:23–15:7	810–785	Israel
Hosea	2 Kgs 15–18	782–725	Israel
Isaiah	2 Kgs 15–20; 2 Chr 26–32	758–698	Judah
Micah	2 Kgs 15:8–20; Isa 7–8; Jer 26:17–19; 2 Chr 27–32	740–630	Judah
Nahum		640–630	Assyria
Zephaniah	2 Kgs 22–23; 2 Chr 34–35	640–610	Judah
Jeremiah	2 Kgs 22–25; 2 Chr 34–36	627–585	Judah
Habbakkuk	2 Kgs 23:31–34; 2 Chr 34–36	608–598	Judah
Daniel	2 Kgs 24–25; 2 Chr 26:5–23	606–534*	Babylon, Persia
Ezekial	2 Kgs 24–25; 2 Chr 26:11–21	592–572	Judah in exile
Obadiah	2 Kgs 25; 2 Chr 26:11–21	586–583	Edom
Haggai	Ezra 1:6	520	Judah
Zechariah	Ezra 1:6	520–518	Judah
Malachi	Neh 7–13	433–425	Judah

This table, developed by W. Graham Scroggie, gives the dates within which the prophet ministered and does not represent the duration of their ministry. *Most scholars now believe the books of Joel, Jonah, and Daniel were written after 500, after 300, and after 200, respectively. Joel seems to have been misdated. Most scholars now believe Jonah and Daniel to have been historical prophets whose legendary feats were used by unknown writers to communicate a message in post-Exilic times.

MEMORABLE COMMENTS

1. Isaiah begins his book by pronouncing the Lord's judgment on Judah, but adds that the Lord has said:

> a. Hard cases make bad law.
> b. Come, let us reason together.
> c. Israel is a horse of a different color.
> d. We write in water.

2. Isaiah extols the power of the Lord, saying that to him the nations of the earth are:

> a. a drop in the bucket
> b. gone with the wind
> c. small beer
> d. but shadows

3. But the day of the Lord will come, and when the messenger comes the watchmen of Jerusalem will:

> a. put all their eggs in one basket
> b. hold a lantern to their shames
> c. see eye to eye
> d. hear sweet music

4. When the Messiah comes, Isaiah foresees, he will be brought:

> a. to the mountaintops of Ephraim
> b. as a lamb to the slaughter
> c. low by vile cunning
> d. as a balm to the righteous

THE APOCRYPHA

The earliest Bible used by the Church was the Greek version produced by the Jewish schools of Alexandria, known as the Septuagint. It included seven books that were not admitted into the Hebrew canon when it was finalized ca. A.D. 90. Jerome in his fourth-century Latin translation included the books but labeled them "libri ecclessiastici" and not "libri canonici" (books of the Church and not books of the canon). Luther included them as an appendix to his German translation in 1534. The King James Version of 1611 included them in a separate section between the Old and New Testaments, following the dictum of the Church of England that they were not doctrine but should be read for instruction. The Catholic and Orthodox Churches continue to regard them as canonical.

Tobit. A very popular story of a pious Jew whose faithfulness amid difficulties results in a visit from the angel Raphael, with wonderful consequences.

Judith. Another in a long line of beautiful Jewish heroines whose encounter with an enemy general leads him, as one critic put it, "first to lose his head over her and then lose his head to her."

First and Second Maccabees. A first-century B.C. history of the second-century revolt against Antiochus Epiphanes and the establishment of the independent Jewish state. Its exhortation to pray for the dead was important in the theological development of purgatory.

Baruch. The writings of Jeremiah's scribe during the Captivity, including a letter from Jeremiah to the captives. Probably a later work.

The Book of Wisdom. A beautiful meditation on wisdom that prefigures much of Christian belief, probably dating from the first century A.D.

Ecclesiasticus, or The Wisdom of Ben-Sira. The philosophical reflections of a great Jewish thinker of the second century B.C. One of the gems of biblical wisdom writing. Also, the wonderful story of **Susanna and the Elders**—a favorite of painters for centuries—is, in the Apocrypha, part of the Book of Daniel.

5. Isaiah's greatest scorn was reserved for those who purported to be:

    a. happy-go-lucky
    b. holier-than-thou
    c. healthy, wealthy, and wise
    d. making hay while the sun shines

6. Jeremiah asks about those who sin but then repent when they realize the Lord's punishment is upon them:

    a. Is this not too little too late?
    b. Is it the empty vessel that makes the loudest sound?
    c. Can a leopard change his spots?
    d. Are you good men and true?

7. The prophet Ezekiel said that people should take responsibility for their own actions and any attempt not to was:

    a. dodging the arrow
    b. sucking eggs
    c. sour grapes
    d. the unkindest cut of all

8. Daniel foresaw that the statue Nebuchadnezzar saw in his dream would fall because it had:

    a. weight upon weight
    b. been built on sand
    c. a crack of idolatry
    d. feet of clay

9. At a banquet, the Babylonian king Belshazzar saw:

    a. the light at the end of the tunnel
    b. the handwriting on the wall
    c. the die is cast
    d. his days were numbered

10. In one of his apocalyptic visions, Daniel saw a great beast with ten horns that "made war with the saints" until the following came:

    a. a woman standing on a crescent
    b. the Great Awakening
    c. the Ancient of days
    d. a bolt of lightning

11. Joel prophesized a day when the Gentiles would need to:

    a. beat their plowshares into swords
    b. welcome home again discarded faith
    c. pluck live lions by the beard
    d. double with deeds their evil words

FAMOUS AND NOT-SO-FAMOUS PEOPLE

12. In his famous taunting of the king of Babylon, Isaiah calls him:

    a. Lucifer   c. Satan
    b. Beelzebub   d. Lilith

13. Isaiah told King Hezekiah that the invader Sennacherib would be diverted by:

a. a plague   c. a rumor
b. a calamity   d. a rebellion

14. According to legend, Isaiah died by being:

a. crucified
b. sawn in half
c. caught up in a whirlwind
d. drowned in the River Jordan

15. When king Zedekiah ignored Jeremiah's warning not to rebel against Babylon, the prophet:

a. cracked the bell of the Temple
b. sent him a basket of thistles
c. made a yoke and wore it
d. fled to the desert

16. The false prophet Hananiah told the king and the people to ignore Jeremiah, and as Jeremiah predicted, he was rewarded with:

a. leprosy
b. death
c. plagues among his children
d. damnation

17. Jeremiah portrayed fallen Israel as being wept over by:

a. the angels   c. David
b. Rachel   d. Jerusalem

18. Jeremiah relied on:

a. his patron Johanan   c. his scribe Baruch
b. his brother Kareath   d. his wife Micah

19. God ordered Hosea to marry a:

a. widow   c. whore
b. sister   d. prophetess

20. In the book of Jonah the only one who fails to obey God is:

a. Jonah   c. the whale
b. the worm   d. Ninevah

PROPHETIC STATEMENTS: TRUE OR FALSE

21. In the last days:

a. the temple will be rebuilt	T	F
b. Israel will again reject the Messiah	T	F
c. the wolf will dwell with the lamb	T	F
d. the nations will keep their languages	T	F
e. no one will be afraid	T	F
f. Jerusalem will be destroyed	T	F
g. people will live a hundred years	T	F
h. wars will increase	T	F
i. Israel will be regathered	T	F
j. David will reign again	T	F

22. The Messiah will:

a. have a forerunner		T	F
b. be born in Bethlehem		T	F
c. deal harshly with the Gentiles		T	F
d. be rejected		T	F
e. ride an ass into Jerusalem		T	F
f. have loyal friends		T	F
g. be buried with the poor		T	F
h. intercede for sinners		T	F
i. be valued at thirty pieces of silver		T	F
j. be worshipped by kings		T	F
k. answer his accusers		T	F
l. be radiant		T	F

CHAPTER 6

THE GOSPELS

≈≈≈

Everything that I have written, every greatness
that has been in any thought of mine, whatever
I have done in my life has been simply due to
the fact that when I was a child my mother daily
read with me a part of the Bible and daily made
me learn a part of it by heart.

—JOHN RUSKIN

OUR EARLIEST HISTORICAL ACCOUNT OF THE GOSPELS—THE
first four books (Matthew, Mark, Luke, and John) of
the New Testament—comes from thirteen fragments
of a work by Papias (ca. A.D. 60–130), a Christian pres-
byter in Asia Minor. According to Irenaeus, bishop of
Lyons in the second century, Papias was "a hearer of
John and a companion of Polycarp, a man of primitive
times." Papias tells us that the author of Mark was
Peter's interpreter (presumably in Rome), who wrote
down the Apostle's memories of the words and actions of Jesus. This Mark has long been traditionally
identified with the John Mark who accompanied Paul
on some of his journeys. Papias also tells us that the
Apostle Matthew organized the sayings of Jesus "in
Hebrew" (which is taken to mean Aramaic) and that
"each one" translated them into various languages.

This slight reference has produced speculation that an earlier Aramaic version of Matthew existed before the final Greek version which we know today.

Mark's gospel is generally believed to have been the first, written before A.D. 68. In recording his gospel, Mark invented an entirely new literary genre, combining biography, narrative, teaching, and revelation. Our word "gospel" is rendered in the original Greek as *euangelion,* or good news, which is more familiar to most of us in its Latin form, *evangelium.* It reached its present form from the Old English "godspel" or "good spiel." The word "gospel" is used 101 times in the King James Version of the New Testament, and only once does it refer to the written account, when John Mark begins his with "This is the gospel of Jesus Christ, the Son of God" (Mark 1:1). On all other occasions it refers to the Christ's message of Redemption, as when first Jesus, then Peter, then Paul "preach the gospel."

Matthew's gospel seems to be a fleshing out of Mark's, with more attention to the teachings of Christ, including the Sermon on the Mount and parables. Indeed, 600 of Mark's 661 verses can be found in Matthew. The gospels of Matthew and Luke seem to have been written about the same time, A.D. 70–80, and they contain portions that are unique to them and not found in Mark. It is generally believed that they shared yet another older source, called the Q Document (for *quelle,* or source). Luke, as well, contains material not found anywhere else, such as the parable of the prodigal son and the story of the good Samaritan. These three—Mark, Matthew, and Luke—are called the Synoptic Gospels because of the similarity of their outlook (*syn-optic,* with one eye). John's gospel, on the other hand, is altogether different in tone, format, and reportage. Yet no matter their similarities, each of the gospels is different in the audiences they were written for and the matters they address.

Matthew was written to a Jewish audience and, from its very first sentence, is written to show that Jesus was the promised Messiah, coming out of the lineage of David as foretold by the prophets. Matthew makes use of a common Jewish practice of referring to Scripture to gain an understanding of a problem. The Jews, relying as they did on a set of injunctions handed down to Moses in the Bronze Age, often found that they had answers for which there were no longer any questions, and questions for which there were no easily identifiable answers. So it was common practice, when confronting a problem, to reconsider and even reinterpret a piece of Scripture as a guideline for how to deal with it. Jesus, of course, presented the biggest problem of all. Was he the Messiah? Matthew guides his readers through several Scriptural citations, asking them to reconsider them in light of Jesus' life. The virgin birth? Reconsider the prophecy of Isaiah regarding Immanuel. The flight to Egypt? Recall Hosea's prophecy, "Out of Egypt will I call my son." The slaughter of the innocents? Rethink Jeremiah's image of Rachel weeping for her children. John the Baptist? Remember Isaiah's "voice crying in the wilderness." Matthew knew his readers were as familiar with Scripture as he was and that some of these citations had never before been considered in the Messianic context. He wants to get them thinking before his main character—Jesus himself—enters onto the stage to speak for himself. And even though Jesus says he has come "not to destroy the Law and the prophets . . . but to fulfill [them]" (Matt 5:17), his own words are clearly an entirely new revelation of what the Law and the prophets were about. Matthew's skill is in presenting Jesus to Jews as a Jew, and not only a Jew, but *the* Jew, the fulfillment of the purpose of the Jewish nation.

Mark is much more straightforward. It is a simple biography whose whole purpose is to teach new Christians in Rome about the incidents that led up to the Passion and Resurrection. Mark's Greek is primitive and sometimes awkward; as rendered in the King James Version and subsequent translations, the gospel's lack of literary merit, paradoxically, is what gives it such a sense of urgency and vitality, as if the writer is fairly bursting with the good news he wants to share with his readers.

Luke is of a very different cast of mind. Tradition has identified its author with Luke, "the beloved physician" mentioned by Paul in his letter to the Colossians. Certainly the author is a well educated and even fluid writer, and his purpose as stated in the prologue is to bring a historian's semiscientific perspective (as it was understood at the time) to the project, and he carefully notes that he has investigated the matters at hand independently, interviewed eyewitnesses to the events, and gained a "perfect understanding" of what transpired in Judaea. He carefully follows the Greek model of biography, and while he owes much to the form devised by Mark and also, it seems, to a source common to Matthew (the Q Document), his version contains much original material. Who, one wonders, was his source for the Annunciation, told in such beautiful detail? Or for the *Magnificat*, Mary's gentle prayer of thanksgiving? If he had

read Matthew, his love of language would surely
have led him to include the Beatitudes in much more
detail than he relates them, so we probably should
assume that he was unaware of the other gospel written at about the same time. He seems less inclined to
argument than Matthew, who was trying to make a
case; Luke's version is more serene and confident, as
if given in perfect faith of its truthfulness—and of its
acceptance by his readers, who undoubtedly included
the members of the young churches he had helped to
found.

John, the last of the Gospels, has been thought for
some eighteen hundred years to also have been the
last written. In the late nineteenth century some scholars, influenced by the evolutionary fashions of the
time, were confidently pronouncing a date for it as
late as A.D. 120, because of its supposedly Hellenistic,
even neo-Platonic, imagery and because its concept of
Christ seemed so highly developed that it must reflect
an "evolved" theology. All the weighty tomes in
which these judgments were pronounced and rea-
soned in minute detail can now be thrown in the rub-
bish heap, for far from being the last of the Gospels, it
now seems possible that John was among the first.
The discovery of the Dead Sea Scrolls and the writings of the Essene community at Qumran show that
John's imagery of light and darkness and his high
Christological treatment of the Messiah were com-
monplace among Jewish thinkers for at least three
hundred years before the birth of Jesus. That, in turn,
means that John had available to him a tradition of
thought and language he could employ in describing
Jesus as the Messiah and in relating Jesus' own belief

in his Christhood. In fact, it could mean that John specifically wrote his gospel with the intention of showing the Essene community that Jesus was the fulfillment of all their own Messianic expectations. In Acts 6:7 we are told that as the number of disciples multiplied in Jerusalem, among them were "a great company of the priests." The three priestly parties at the time were the Sadducees, the Pharisees, and the Essenes. The Sadducees were rigorous in their devotion to the Mosaic Law and did not believe in the concept of resurrection, so they were unlikely converts. The Pharisees were the chief persecutors of Jesus and had plotted his death. That leaves the Essenes as candidates for conversion, and John himself —who is thought to have been "the beloved disciple" but is described in the gospel only as an eyewitness— may have been closely connected to them.

A word here is probably in order about the caves at Qumran and the importance of the discoveries made there. At the northwestern end of the Dead Sea in 1947, a number of scrolls were found in a cave. Subsequent excavations of the area, which continue to this day, unearthed all the books of the Old Testament except Esther, and many other documents and fragments of documents of a religious nature. The caves were sealed, and some of the documents and scrolls destroyed, by a Roman legion in A.D. 68 during the tumultuous rebellion against Rome which lasted from A.D. 66 until the final defeat of the Jewish partisans and the destruction of the Temple in A.D. 70. It is widely believed that the scrolls were hidden in the caves to protect them during the rebellion, although in the vicinity archeologists have uncovered the remains of buildings thought to have been the center of an Essene community. Of chief importance to Christians among the discoveries are not only such documents as "The War of the Sons of Light Against the Sons of Darkness"—an apocalyptic work and only one of many that use the imagery associated with John's gospel—but also a fragment identified as a portion of Mark's gospel and another fragment which computer analysis in 1991 identified as a portion of Paul's first letter to Timothy. Like John's gospel, this letter has long been thought to be a latter development, probably not written by Paul at all, because it refers to such ecclesiastical matters as the naming of bishops, which scholars thought too complex an organizational matter for the early stages of the Church. However, if this discovery holds up, it means that the letter, like Mark's gospel, was definitely written sometime before the caves were sealed in A.D. 68.

All in all, these discoveries show the wisdom of Pope Pius XII's instruction in 1943 to encourage historical research into the Bible and its authors, a move widely credited with spurring investigation not only among Catholic scholars, but among Jews and Protestants as well. Far from having anything to fear from such research, the Christian Church has everything to gain from increased scholarship, and from the newer methods of linguistic analysis and computer modeling which have enabled us to glean more precise knowledge of issues long thought settled. We are not likely to ever know everything we would like about the Gospels and other writings of the New Testament, but every bit we add to our knowledge only confirms and strengthens the faith which they proclaim.

THE MOST FAMOUS ANGELS
OF THEM ALL

Angels are mentioned 273 times in 34 books of the canonical Bible, but only three are named. The Archangels Michael and Gabriel are mentioned five times each. The record holder is none other than the Great Deceiver himself: Satan is mentioned by name fifty-five times.

SELECTED READINGS:
Matthew, Mark, Luke, and John.

Answers begin on page 187.

MEMORABLE COMMENTS

1. In the Sermon on the Mount, Jesus admonishes his followers to:

      a. make a virtue of necessity
      b. burn the candle at both ends
      c. beware of wolves in sheep's clothing
      d. turn over a new leaf

2. In the same sermon Jesus sought to inspire his followers with a new vision of their place in God's kingdom. He said to them that they were:

      a. the best and the brightest
      b. babes in the woods

c. the salt of the earth
d. chips off the old block

3. When Jesus first began his ministry, his old friends and neighbors were incredulous at the sudden change in someone they had known so long, and they said to one another that he was:

a. out on a limb
b. beside himself
c. on the path to perdition
d. on the side of the angels

4. When Jesus first preached at his hometown synagogue, he quoted this proverb:

a. To err is human, to forgive divine.
b. When one door shuts, another opens.
c. Bite not the hand that feeds you.
d. Physician, heal thyself.

THE FISH

It is not known how the fish became the earliest Christian symbol for Christ, although it is certainly well attested to in catacomb drawings and in writings of the early Church Fathers. It is thought to have come from the acrostic in Greek that results from the first letters of "Jesus Christ, Son of God, Savior"—which is *ichthus,* fish—but the acrostic could have just as easily come from the symbol.

5. When Jesus first cast out demons, he was challenged by the scribes from Jerusalem, who said such power could come only from Satan. Jesus asked, "How can Satan cast out Satan?" and went on to say:

> a. These words are sharper than a serpent's tooth.
> b. A house divided against itself cannot stand.
> c. This is the pot calling the kettle black.
> d. You hypocrites will be hoisted on your own petard.

6. Jesus often used metaphors and parables to make his point. In answering questions put to him by the Pharisees, he said:

> a. Bend the tree when it is young.
> b. You can't judge a tree by its bark.
> c. You can tell a tree by its fruit.
> d. In a tempest beware the tree.

7. In another confrontation with the Pharisees, Jesus quoted an old adage:

> a. Never look a gift horse in the mouth.
> b. Red sky at night, the day will be bright.
> c. Bad herdsmen ruin their flocks.
> d. You can't make a silk purse out of a sow's ear.

8. In one parable, Jesus told of a king who prepared a lavish wedding feast for his son, but the guests didn't show up. The king sent servants out to round up anyone they could find to attend. When one of the

newly invited guests came wearing inappropriate
clothes, the king had him tossed out, saying:

> a. Clothes make the man.
> b. This adds insult to injury.
> c. Do not play with fire.
> d. Many are called, but few are chosen.

9. Jesus told the parable of the complacent rich man
who had a great harvest and said to himself:

> a. Make hay while the sun shines.
> b. That's icing on the cake.
> c. Eat, drink, and be merry.
> d. A bird in the hand is worth two in the
>   bush.

10. After raising Lazarus from the dead, Jesus
stayed with him and his sisters Mary and Martha.
One night Mary washed Jesus' feet with an expensive
ointment, causing Judas Iscariot to complain, and
Jesus to answer:

> a. Charity begins at home.
> b. Cleanliness is next to Godliness.
> c. God helps those who help themselves.
> d. The poor are with you always.

FAMOUS PEOPLE

11. Only four women are mentioned in Matthew's
genealogy of Christ. Who is *not* among them?

a. Sarah   c. Tamar
b. Rahab   d. Ruth

12. *Jesus* in Hebrew means:

a. Immanuel   c. God with us
b. Salvation   d. Son of Joseph

13. Zachariah, the father of John the Baptist, didn't believe the announcement of the Angel Gabriel and as punishment he was:

a. struck dumb   c. paralyzed
b. made impotent   d. blinded

14. Joseph, when he first learned that Mary was pregnant, decided to:

    a. flee from Nazareth
    b. terminate their betrothal
    c. send her away to her cousin Elizabeth
    d. marry her quickly

SALOME AND
THE DANCE OF THE SEVEN VEILS

The New Testament never mentions Salome. Matthew and Mark say only that "the daughter of Herodias" danced before Herod. It was Josephus, a first-century Jewish historian, who identified Herodias' daughter as Salome. The Gospels say only that she danced before the king. The sensual "Dance of the Seven Veils" was invented by Richard Strauss for his opera *Salome*, first performed in 1905.

15. When John the Baptist saw Jesus for the first time, he called him:

a. the Lamb of God   c. the beloved Son
b. the Savior of Israel   d. the Messiah

16. According to the three Synoptic Evangelists, he was the second apostle, and according to John he was the first. Who was he?

a. Simon   c. Andrew
b. Philip   d. John

17. The first person Jesus raised from the dead was:

a. Jairus' daughter   c. Peter's mother-in-law
b. Lazarus   d. the widow's son

18. Jesus gave Simon the nickname of Cephas, which means:

a. strong-headed   c. cornerstone
b. rock   d. rash

19. Jesus seemed to like nicknames. He called James and John, the two sons of Zebedee, *Boanerges*, which means:

a. first servers   c. sons of thunder
b. kinsmen   d. men of virtue

20. When the Pharisees upbraided Jesus for allowing his disciples to pluck ears of grain on the Sabbath, he cited as a precedent the example of:

a. Moses and the manna   c. Gideon and the dew
b. David and the   d. Samson and the
   shewbread   honey

21. Among the women who ministered to and helped to feed the disciples was Mary, called Magdalene, who had been:

a. healed of demons   c. married four times
b. a prostitute   d. wealthy

22. When Jesus was asked for a sign, he replied that no sign would be given except for the sign of the prophet:

a. Hosea   c. Daniel
b. Isaiah   d. Jonah

23. When Herod heard about the fame of Jesus, he said that Jesus must be:

a. Elijah   c. a demon
b. John the Baptist   d. Elisha

24. When Jesus came into the country of the Gerasenes, he confronted a man possessed by demons. When Jesus asked him for his name, he replied that his name was:

a. Beelzebub   c. Legion
b. Dementia   d. Damned

25. On entering a village, Jesus was met by ten lepers, and when he sent them to the priests, the lepers found on the way that they had been healed. But only one returned to thank Jesus. He was:

a. a Samaritan   c. the only righteous Jew
b. the least devout   d. a Nazarene

26. On entering Jericho, Jesus decided to dine at the house of Zacchaeus, who was:

a. ruler of the synagogue   c. a Pharisee
b. the chief tax collector   d. a felon

27. When the rulers first attempted to arrest Jesus on a charge of blasphemy, they were stopped when one of their own demanded he be given a fair trial. This Pharisee was:

a. Hilliel   c. Joseph of Arimathea
b. Nicodemus   d. Gamiliel

28. Pilate was warned to have nothing to do with Jesus' death by:

a. his centurian   c. his augurs
b. his wife   d. his legal adviser

29. When Jesus was captured and brought to trial, the chief argument that it was expedient that one man should die for the people was put to the Sanhedrin by:

a. Caiaphas   c. Herod Antipas
b. Annas   d. Malchus

30. According to John, one of the disciples was missing when Jesus first appeared after his Resurrection. It was:

a. John   c. Thomas
b. Matthew   d. Philip

WHAT AND WHY

31. Joseph fled to Egypt to escape Herod's massacre of the innocents. When Joseph learned in a dream of Herod's death, he led his family out of Egypt, and settled them in:

a. Galilee   c. Samaria
b. Judaea   d. Peraea

32. When Mary and Joseph brought the infant Jesus to be presented at the Temple, they offered a sacrifice of:

a. a newborn lamb   c. an ephah of flour
b. two turtledoves   d. a log of oil

33. Matthew cites a number of Old Testament prophecies relating to the coming of the Messiah. However, he seems to have gotten carried away. Which prophecy did Matthew quote which does *not* exist in the Old Testament?

a. The Messiah would come out of Bethlehem of Judah.
b. Galilee of the Gentiles will see the light.
c. The Messiah will be called a Nazarene.
d. A virgin shall bring forth a son that will be called Emmanuel.

THE FOUR LISTS OF THE DISCIPLES

The New Testament gives four lists of the names of the original disciples. The differences among the versions are thought to be caused by confusions arising from patronymics, nicknames, and conversion names.

Matthew's List. Simon, called Peter; Andrew, his brother; James, the son of Zebedee; John, his brother; Philip; Bartholomew; Thomas; Matthew, the publican; James, the son of Alphaeus; Lebbaeus, whose surname was Thaddaeus; Simon, the Cannanite; and Judas Iscariot. (10:2–4)

Mark's List. Simon, surnamed Peter; James, the son of Zebedee; John, the brother of James; Andrew; Philip; Bartholomew; Matthew; Thomas; James, the son of Alphaeus; Thaddeus; Simon, the Cannanite; Judas Iscariot. (3:16–19)

Luke's List. Simon (whom he also named Peter); Andrew, his brother; James; John; Philip; Bartholomew; Matthew; Thomas; James, the son of Alphaeus; Simon, called Zelotes; Judas, the brother of James; and Judas Iscariot. (6:14–16)

Acts' List. Peter; James; John; Andrew; Philip; Thomas; Bartholomew; Matthew; James, the son of Alphaesus, Simon Zelotes, and Judas, the brother of James. (1:13)

As might be expected from two works by the same author, Luke and Acts come closest to agreement, varying only in precedence.

34. Which was *not* one of the temptations Satan offered to Christ?

    a. turn the stones into bread
    b. cast himself off the pinnacle
    c. have dominion over all the kingdoms
    d. sit on the Throne of Glory

35. According to Mark, Jesus was first recognized as the Christ by:

a. Mary   c. a leper
b. Peter   d. a demon

36. According to John, Jesus performed his first miracle reluctantly, at the request of:

a. Peter   c. a centurion
b. a blind man   d. Mary

37. At Jacob's Well in Samaria, Jesus encountered a woman who had:

a. five husbands   c. the prophetic gift
b. leprosy   d. seven children

38. The Pharisees hated Jesus because he:

    a. fed the people for free
    b. cured a lame man on the Sabbath
    c. prophesied about the coming of the Kingdom
    d. gathered so many supporters

39. Many of Jesus' disciples left him when he said:

    a. Whoso eateth my flesh, and drinketh my blood, hath eternal life.
    b. Think not that I am come to send peace on earth: I came not to send peace, but a sword.
    c. Except a man be born again, he cannot see the kingdom of God.
    d. It is easier for a camel to go through the

eye of a needle, than for a rich man to
enter into the kingdom of God.

40. John's gospel contains the Seven Great *I Am*
Sayings, by which Jesus defined himself for his disciples. Try to fill in the correct missing word in each:

a. I am the _____ of life.
b. I am the _____ of the world.
c. I am the _____ of the sheep.
d. I am the good _____.
e. I am the _____ and the life.
f. I am the way, the _____, and
the life.
g. I am the true _____.

WHO WAS THE FIRST SAINT?

Roman Catholic tradition defines a saint as a person so
faultless that he or she is taken directly into heaven without any intervening time in purgatory. By that definition,
the first saint must have been the "good thief" to whom
Jesus said, "Today shalt thou be with me in paradise"
(Luke 23:43). (He is traditionally known as St. Ditmas, and
his feast day in the Roman calendar is March 25.)

THE BEATITUDES

41. See how well you remember the Beatitudes by
filling in the appropriate words:

a. Blessed are the _____:
for theirs is the kingdom of heaven.
b. Blessed are they that _____: for
they shall be comforted.
c. Blessed are the _____: for they
shall inherit the earth.
d. Blessed are they which _____:
for they shall be filled.
e. Blessed are the _____: for they
shall obtain mercy.
f. Blessed are the _____: for they
shall see God.
g. Blessed are the _____: for they
shall be called the children of God.
h. Blessed are they which are
_____: for theirs is the kingdom
of heaven.
i. Blessed are ye, when _____, and
persecute you, and shall say all manner
of evil against you falsely, for my sake.
j. Rejoice and be exceeding glad: for great
is _____: for so persecuted they
the prophets which were before you.

THE SERMON ON THE MOUNT:
MATTHEW 5–7

See how many of these familiar phrases from the
Sermon on the Mount you can complete:

42. Ye are the light _____ .

43. And if thy right eye offend thee, _____ _____ .

44. But whosoever shall smite thee on thy right cheek, _____ .

45. And whosoever shall compel thee to go a mile, _____ .

46. But lay up for yourselves treasures _____ _____ .

47. Ye cannot serve God _____ .

48. Which one of you by taking thought can add _____ ?

49. Sufficient unto the day is the _____ _____ .

50. Judge not, that _____ .

51. Neither cast ye your pearls _____ _____ .

52. Ask, and it _____ .

53. What man is there of you, whom if his son ask bread, will he give him _____ ?

54. Whatsoever ye would that men should do to you, do _____ .

55. Ye shall know them by _____.

56. Therefore whosoever heareth these sayings of mine, and doeth them, I will liken him unto a wise man, which built _____.

THE PARABLES

57. In the parable of the wheat, Jesus told of a man who sowed good seed in his field, but his enemy came along and:

a. sowed weeds   c. set traps
b. raked it up   d. reaped his grain

58. Jesus likened the kingdom of heaven to many things. Which is *not* among them?

a. a treasure hid in a   c. a grain of mustard
   field   seed
b. a net   d. a camel

59. In one parable, a householder hires a first group of workers in the morning and a second group in the afternoon, and when the day was done he:

a. paid each according to his labor
b. paid all the same
c. refused to pay the afternoon laborers
d. gave all the laborers a bonus

60. Another householder hired husbandmen for his vineyard, and went to a far country. When it was time

for the harvest to be collected, he sent his servants, who were beaten, stoned, and even killed. Finally when he sent his son to collect:

    a. they gave over the harvest
    b. they killed him
    c. they fled
    d. they begged forgiveness

61. In another parable, Jesus likened the kingdom of heaven to ten virgins, five of whom were wise and five of whom were foolish, who were waiting to welcome a bridegroom to his marriage feast. The five foolish virgins:

    a. fell asleep
    b. forgot their lamps
    c. went off to buy oil for their lamps
    d. went to the wrong house

62. In the parable of the talents, Jesus told of a man traveling to a far country who split his wealth among three servants, giving five talents to one, two talents to another, and one talent to the third. Only the third buried his for safety, while the other two invested theirs. Which did Jesus condemn?

    a. the two that invested theirs
    b. the third that buried his

63. In the parable of the rich man and the beggar Lazarus, each died, and the rich man went to hell while the beggar went to heaven. When the rich man begged Abraham to send the beggar to his brothers so

that they would be warned about the torments that awaited the unjust, Abraham replied:

    a. Not even someone risen from the dead would convince them.

    b. The rich man should pray for his brothers.

    c. They are already condemned so it would be no use.

    d. He should have thought about his brothers when he was alive.

64. In the parable of the unjust judge, Jesus told of how a widow who had been wronged finally achieved justice from the magistrate by:

    a. selling her goods for two pence and bribing him

    b. continually importuning him

    c. convincing him of her case

    d. throwing herself on his mercy

CHAPTER 7

THE
APOSTOLIC
WRITINGS

≈≈≈

The period of the Reformation was a judgment
day for Europe, when all the nations were presented with an open Bible, and all the emanci-
pation of heart and intellect which an open Bible involves.

—THOMAS CARLYLE

THE WRITINGS OF THE APOSTLES CONSIST OF ACTS, THE
Epistles, and Revelation—history, doctrine, and
prophecy. The Gospels are about Christ, and the Apostolic Writings are about his Church. The Gospels
give us the facts about Christ's life and teaching; the
Apostolic Writings interpret those facts through the
prism of each author's particular gifts and understanding. The Gospels reveal the truth, and the Apostolic Writings reveal the faith through which the truth
is kept alive. In the Gospels we read how Christ gave
his message to the disciples. In the Apostolic Writings
we read how the disciples gave his message to the
world.

The *Acts of the Apostles* is undoubtedly the work of
Luke, the author of the Third Gospel, and it continues
in the historical vein as history writing was under-

stood at the time. One requirement of an ancient historian, for example, was that he be well traveled, and Luke took some pains to show that he participated in the missionary voyages. He follows the pattern set by the Roman historians Sallust and Livy as well as the great Greek Thucydides in using orations by his chief characters Peter and Paul to move the story along as well as to explain its meaning. The accuracy of Luke's history in those places where it coincides with secular history has been fairly well documented by archeological discoveries and other ancient sources. Luke's history begins with the Ascension of Christ and ends with the imprisonment of Paul in Rome but before his martyrdom, which occurred in A.D. 67. One of the mysteries of Acts is its abrupt ending. It does not include the deaths of either Paul or Peter. Since Acts was written after Luke, and Luke was written sometime between A.D. 70 and 80, the best surmise is that the author himself may have died before he was able to reach the climax of his story in the martyrdoms of the two great central characters of his narrative.

Acts can be divided into three parts. In chapters 1–7, the Apostles are centered in Jerusalem, and their message is to a restored Israel. In chapters 8–12, the Church begins to broaden its appeal with Philip's mission to Samaria, Peter's miracles in Lydda and Joppa and his conversion of the Roman Cornelius, and Barnabas' mission to Antioch. In chapters 13–28, Paul takes center stage with his missionary efforts among the Greeks.

The *Epistles* are usually divided into the thirteen *Pauline Epistles* and the eight *Catholic Epistles*. Of the latter, the canon has accepted one from Jude, one from James, two from Peter, and three from John. The

Letter to the Hebrews is of unknown authorship, and has been variously attributed to Barnabas, Clement of Rome, Priscilla, and others.

W. Graham Scroggie has written of the authors, "Paul is the Apostle of Gentile Christianity; James and Jude, of Jewish Christianity; Peter, of Catholic Christianity; and John, of Mystical Christianity." These are the principal schools of thought or communities of faith in which early orthodox Christianity was nourished, and despite the tensions among them, their cross-pollination was essential for the growth of the Church. Not all the letters attributed in the canon to the respective Apostles can be positively identified as having been written by them, but are thought to have come from the communities which followed them. The second and third letters of John, for example, are thought to have been written by John the Elder, a leader of the community founded by the Apostle John. Of the *Pauline Letters*, the letter to the Ephesians, first and second Timothy, and Titus have long been regarded as not directly from Paul's hand, although a computer analysis of a fragment found at Qumran has identified it as first Timothy and therefore authentically Pauline.

In these letters we can discern the doctrines of the Church, and since they preceded the Gospels by decades in most cases, from them we get our fullest understanding of early Christianity. They reveal that the orthodoxy of the Church was fully established at its very beginning. In first Corinthians, for example, Paul says about the Lord's Supper, "For I have received of the Lord that which also I delivered unto you, That the Lord Jesus the same night in which he was betrayed took bread . . ." (1 Cor 11:23). James in his letter gives a summary of the Sermon on the Mount so close to Matthew's, written thirty years later, that the points can be paralleled. But the beauty of the Epistles is that they are not dry doctrinal treatises, or theological theorems, or rationalistic ethical arguments, but letters—and as letters they reveal the personalities of their authors. They give us Christianity not as an abstract system but as a living, heartfelt, and faith-filled way of life.

I. *Pauline Epistles*

"No other letters ever written have begun to have the influence of those produced by Paul of Tarsus as an adjunct to his missionary labors," wrote the critic Ernest Sutherland Bates. "Composed to meet the specific needs of particular congregations established by him, occasional in their utterance, adapted to local times and places, they nevertheless often touched upon themes of such universal religious influence and treated them in so profound a manner—yet always with the special organization of the church in mind— that they became the prime factor in the development of both the inner and outer aspects of Christianity as at once a subjective attitude of spirit and an objective institution."

The canonical presentation of Paul's letters is not in sequence; for purposes of this discussion we will list them in what is generally regarded as chronological order.

First Thessalonians was written after Paul had been driven from Thessalonia (Acts 17:10) to comfort and encourage the young church he had founded there. It is filled with joy that his converts have remained faithful even during their trials, and with anxiety for their spiritual well-being. It is Paul at his paternal best.

Second Thessalonians seeks to correct a misunderstanding which grew up among some in the congregation about the Second Coming. He urges them to "hold the traditions" which they have been taught, which include the teaching of the anti-Christ which must precede the Lord's appearance.

Galatians is a defense of Paul's own broad and inclusive brand of Christianity against a Judaizing element in the early Church (apparently even more hard line than James) that regarded the Christian revelation as an exclusively Jewish property.

First Corinthians is a response to questions put to him by the church in Corinth regarding various practices and beliefs. Paul uses the opportunity to call the congregation to a higher understanding of the spiritual gifts it has received. While *Galatians* might be seen as an expression of Pauline dogma, *First Corinthians* gives expression to Pauline ethics, and it includes incomparable passages on the Lord's Supper, the Body of Christ, the nature of love, and the Resurrection.

Second Corinthians contains such sharp shifts in mood that it has long been supposed to be a compilation of three different letters sent at different times to quell a controversy similar to the one in Galatia that has broken out in the Corinthian church. In it, Paul reveals every facet of his multifaceted personality: he is alternately disparaging and encouraging, joyful and despairing, turbulent and calm, wrathful and paternal.

Romans was written from Corinth at the height of Paul's Apostolic career, and it is his most profound systematic theological and philosophical exposition of the Christian faith.

Philippians is the first of Paul's prison letters, and it seems the most spontaneous. An old man now, weary from his exertions, tired of controversy, headed almost certainly for martyrdom, Paul writes with simple sympathy and deep joy.

Colossians is written from Rome to a young church Paul did not found to aid it in warding off the twin heresies of the early Church: Judaism, which held that Christians must follow the Mosaic Law; and Gnosticism, which held that Christian knowledge was the exclusive privilege of a select few initiated into Christian mysteries.

Ephesians is very different from Paul's other epistles; it seems to have been a circular letter meant to be sent around to all the churches of Asia Minor. It seems unlikely that Paul would have written a letter to Ephesus where he lived for three years and make no personal references at all. This has led to speculation that it was sent out from Paul's followers in Rome to the young churches, perhaps after his death, and his name was only attached to it later.

Philemon was handwritten by Paul to his friend Philemon on behalf of Philemon's slave, Onesimus, whom Paul converted while in prison.

First Timothy and the other Pastoral Letters, *Titus* and *Second Timothy*, have been objected to because they reflect a more highly evolved ecclesiastical organization than was thought possible for the first-century Church. However, it is not possible to conceive of a man of Paul's acknowledged genius founding independent churches and leaving them to their own devices, to sink or swim, without any organizational connection or guidance to protect them, especially considering the controversies and heresies that had already sprouted within them. The fragment discovered in Qumran which confirms the validity of these letters as Pauline remains subject to investigation, but it only confirms what many Church historians have thought to be true from the start.

II. *Epistle to the Hebrews*

The *Epistle to the Hebrews*, like many books of the Old Testament to which it refers, is of unknown authorship. It is certainly not Paul's, even though it was attributed to him in early editions of the King James Version. It may not have been a letter at all, but a series of closely connected sermons. Whoever the author, he (or she, for it may be the only book in the Bible written by a woman) is a formidable thinker and an expressive writer. The epistle is aimed at Jewish Christians, probably in Rome. Its major theological premise is the fulfillment of the Old Covenant in the New, but it also counsels patience against the tribulations which the Roman church was enduring at the time.

III. *Catholic Epistles*

These epistles are "catholic" or "universal" because they were meant for general distribution and were not addressed to particular congregations as were the letters of Paul. It may also mean that they contain "Catholic" or "orthodox" doctrine. The designation was first made in the time of Clement of Alexandria in the third century.

James may be the earliest book in the New Testament, written before the Council of Jerusalem which took place in A.D. 44 or 45. There are no fewer than five Jameses referred to among the early disciples: (1)

the son of Zebedee and brother of John (Mark 1:19); (2) the son of Alphaeus (Mark 3:18); (3) the brother of Jesus (Mark 6:3, Gal 1:19); (4) "the Less" (Mark 15:40); and (5) "the brother of Jude" (Jude 1). The second and fourth probably refer to the same person, as do the third and fifth, so that brings us down to three: James, the son of Zebedee; James, the son of Alphaeus; and James, the brother of Jesus and Jude. This epistle was written by the latter James, who converted after Jesus' death and was Bishop of Jerusalem. This James, like most of the original Apostles, remained a Jew (indeed, he is said to have spent so much time in the Temple praying that his knees were calloused), and if he himself wouldn't have anything to do with Gentiles, as the Law required, he at least approved Paul's missionary efforts among them (Acts 15:19). His epistle is vigorous and straightforward; it breathes new life into the ancient Wisdom writings of the Jews by injecting them with the new spirit of Christianity.

First Peter was written by, or in the name of, the Apostle Peter in Rome. Although from earliest times it has been considered authoritative (in the third century the Christian scholar Eusebius said it was the only book about which there was no controversy), the distinction between authority and authorship did not preoccupy the ancient mind as it does the modern. The letter was written on Peter's authority, and that was that. It was written to reassure the churches of Asia of the bonds of suffering, faith, and hope which the church in Rome shared with them and to remind them of their unity.

Second Peter was written to refute novel heresies of the early second century and to reinforce the unifying Christian message by appealing to tradition and by recalling the promises of Christ. Since it was seemingly written after Peter's death, the letter was barely accepted into the canon. From a historical point of view, it—along with the noncanonical letters of Clement, a successor of Peter—is an expression of the confidence of the early Roman church in its reliance upon Petrine authority in correcting abuses in the Church after the age of the Apostles.

First John undoubtedly comes from the hand of the author of the Fourth Gospel. He denounces those who would dispute the dual nature of Christ as both human and divine, but he does so with an understanding that is mystical and in language that is gentle and benign.

Second John and *Third John* are unlike the other *Catholic Epistles* in that they are addressed to specific individuals and are almost domestic in their simplicity. They were probably written by a disciple of the Apostle, also named John and known as John the Elder.

Jude refers to himself as the "brother of James," which is taken to mean James, the brother of Jesus and leader of the Jerusalem church, in which case Jude was also the brother of Jesus. That he does not mention this connection may be a mark of humility or of reverence. His letter is a direct assault on "false teachers" who have "crept in unawares" to confound the early Church with theories and evil practices.

Revelation is not properly an Apostolic writing, since it seems to have been written by a John other than the Apostle, a Christian prophet exiled to the island of Patmos. (Its Greek does not come close to the fluency of the Fourth Gospel or First John.) It is not Apostolic in another sense either, for it does not purport to teach. Rather it is Apocalyptic, and in its vision of "a new heaven and a new earth" is the appropriate ending to the Bible which begins with the Creation of heaven and the earth. Written to seven churches of Asia Minor, it contains an almost cinematic profusion of colors, images, intonations, musical instruments, and forms. Its prophetic insight into the end times has too often been confused with foresight, which has led every generation since it was written to find in it a forecast of the end of the world. It would probably be better if more people in reading it kept in mind Richard Moulton's advice that "in interpreting symbolism the first critical requirement is restraint." After translating it from Greek into Latin, St. Jerome said, "Revelation contains as many mysteries as it does words." Nevertheless, the reader is well rewarded for the trouble of tackling it, for the sheer magnificence of its poetic power.

The Apostolic Writings are the great gift of the early Church to the present Church, the living testimony of those who were often eyewitnesses to the acts of Christ himself and who first endured the trial of taking up his cross and following him. This was not a task for the weak in spirit: tradition tells us that all twelve of the disciples were martyred. The thirty-one successors to Peter as head of the church in Rome over two hundred and fifty years were executed. Christian property was confiscated, children were taken from their parents, many suffered horrible deaths, and many others were tortured or exiled. Even amid such persecution the Church continued to grow, emboldened by the example and teachings of its earliest leaders as given in these books and letters.

SELECTED READINGS:
Acts, the Pauline Letters, Epistle to the Hebrews, Revelation.

Answers begin on page 204.

MEMORABLE COMMENTS

1. When Peter commanded that the Gentiles of Cornelius' household be baptized, he said he did it because God:

>   a. is no respecter of persons
>   b. disposes what man proposes
>   c. moves in mysterious ways
>   d. is love

2. Paul was wary of making too much of himself, and he was thankful that he had been given:

>   a. the gift of laughter
>   b. a thorn in the flesh
>   c. a dark night of the soul
>   d. the way of the Cross

3. Paul constantly reminded his converts to resist the blandishments of the world, at one point warning:

>   a. Deceit is the devil's delight.
>   b. Charity begins at home.
>   c. Money is the root of all evil.
>   d. Where there's smoke, there's fire.

4. Commenting on the trials endured by the new Christians, James urges them to show:

a. grace under pressure
b. the patience of Job
c. one good turn deserves another
d. a stiff upper lip

PERIPATETIC PAUL

First Missionary Journey: From Antioch to Attalia, Perga, Antioch of Pisidia, Iconium, Lystra, and Derbe, all of which were cities in Asia Minor, and the island of Cyprus. (Acts 13–14)
Second Missionary Journey: From Antioch to Tarsus (Paul's hometown), Nicaea, Troas, and across the Aegean Sea to Neapolis, Thessalonia, Berea, Athens, Corinth, and back across the Aegean to Ephesus, along the coast to Cos and Rhodes, and on to Jerusalem. (Acts 15–18)
Third Missionary Journey: From Antioch to revisit churches in Asia Minor, then to Greece. New cities visited include Assos, Mitylene, Miletus, Patara, and Myra before returning to Jerusalem via Tyre. (Acts 18–21)

MIXED SIGNALS

In Galatians 6:2, Paul writes, "Bear ye one another's burdens . . ." Three verses later, he says, ". . . every man shall bear his own burden." No contradiction, really, but three verses apart?

5. The author of Hebrews reminds his readers to be hospitable to strangers, because:

a. some have entertained angels unawares
b. when helping others we can do no harm ourselves

c. one good turn asketh another
d. enough is as good as a feast

6. Paul said the Second Coming would occur:

a. when you least expect it
b. in the twinkling of an eye
c. when the time is ripe
d. like a benediction from on high

7. When the Risen Lord appeared to Saul on the road to Damascus, he said it was hard for Saul to:

a. kick against the pricks
b. believe the evidence of his own eyes
c. bequeath his all to God
d. be true to himself

8. Paul cautioned that Christians should be subject to:

a. the law of love
b. the powers that be
c. the still, small voice
d. the laws of the land

9. Jason, who had housed Paul and Silas in Thessalonia, was hauled before the magistrates by a crowd who said the disciples had:

a. turned the world upside down
b. made a mountain out of a molehill
c. turned day into night
d. to give the devil his due

10. After Paul defended himself before Festus the Roman governor, Festus said:

> a. All men have faults, and honesty is his.
> b. Prepare to meet thy Maker.
> c. Much learning doth make thee mad.
> d. Mend thy speech or mar thy fortunes.

FAMOUS PEOPLE
(AND SOME THAT OUGHT TO BE)

11. To replace Judas Iscariot among the Twelve, the Disciples selected:

a. Barnabas   c. Matthias
b. Nicodemus   d. Paul

12. When Ananias and his wife Sapphira held back part of the money they had promised to give to the fledgling Christian community, they:

> a. were excommunicated
> b. quickly realized their error and gave it all back
> c. were struck dead
> d. decided they didn't want to be Christians after all

13. When Peter and the apostles were hauled before the Sanhedrin for the second time, the rulers were ready to execute them, but were stopped by the moderating speech of:

a. Gamiliel   c. Hilliel
b. Caiphas   d. Annas

14. The first Christian martyr was:

a. Peter   c. Philip
b. Stephen   d. Matthias

15. When Philip preached to the Samaritans, he converted many to the gospel, but when Peter came to confirm their baptisms, one convert used the occasion to try to buy Apostolic office. Who was he?

a. Simon   c. Aristus
b. Jonathan   d. Marcus

16. By legend Philip converted an entire nation when he interpreted the prophecies of Isaiah to:

a. a queen   c. a sultan
b. a eunuch   d. a chieftain

17. In Damascus, Saul was baptized into the faith he had persecuted by:

a. Barnabus   c. Ananias
b. Matthias   d. Peter

18. The second martyr of the faith was:

a. Alchaeus   c. James, the brother of John
b. James, the brother of Jesus   d. Barnabus

19. When Peter was miraculously released from prison, he went to the house of Mary, the mother of:

a. Jesus   c. James
b. John Mark   d. Jude

20. When Paul and Barnabus preached the gospel to the proconsul of Paphos, they were confronted by:

a. a sorcerer   c. Herod's captain
b. the ruler of the   d. a witch
   synagogue

21. The first convert to Christianity in Europe was:

a. Priscilla   c. Lydia
b. Marcellus   d. Justus

YOU ARE WHAT YOU READ

Paul's Epistle to the Romans may be the most important letter ever written. After opening his Bible to it and putting his finger on verse 13:13, Augustine abandoned a life of hedonism and converted to Christianity. Luther found in verses 1:16–17 his doctrine of justification by faith alone. John Calvin found in it his doctrine of double predestination. On hearing Luther's introduction to it read from the pulpit on May 24, 1738, John Wesley underwent a conversion experience, and later he depended on it for his teaching of sanctification by grace.

---

22. Paul and Silas were beaten and imprisoned in Philippi when Paul:

a. compared himself to Mercury
b. cast the demon out of a soothsayer
c. healed a lame man
d. prayed for thunder and lightning

23. In Athens, despite the skepticism with which he was received, Paul converted Dionysius the Areopagite, who was:

a. the ruler of the synagogue
b. a believer in the Unknown God
c. a member of the Athenian council
d. a leading Roman philosopher

24. When Paul made his defense before the court in Caesura, he almost converted:

a. Festus   c. Felix
b. Bernice   d. Agrippa

25. In Melita (Malta) Paul was bitten by a:

a. viper   c. horse
b. shark   d. possessed man

26. The first letter to the Corinthians was written to the young church in Corinth by Paul and:

a. Timothy   c. Barnabus
b. Sosthenes   d. Sopater

27. In the first letter to the Corinthians, Paul condemns the divisions that have separated the church into followers of himself or Peter or Christ or:

a. Apollos   c. Philip
b. James   d. Aquila

28. The writer of Hebrews conceives of Jesus as the ideal high priest, consecrated according to the order of:

a. David   c. Melchizedek
b. Abraham   d. Aaron

WHAT AND WHY

29. When the Holy Spirit descended upon the apostles at Pentecost, it first enabled them to:

a. foresee the future   c. cast out demons
b. speak in other   d. heal the sick
   languages

30. Peter's first miracle after being filled with the Spirit was to:

a. restore sight to a blind   c. strike dead an accuser
   man
b. heal a lame man   d. resurrect a dead child

31. The Apostles asked the early community in Jerusalem to choose from themselves seven men who would:

a. become missionaries to the rest of Judaea
b. devote themselves to prayer and fasting
c. negotiate with the Jewish authorities
d. minister to the community's daily needs

32. Peter commanded the Gentiles of Cornelius' household be baptized after they:

    a. fell on their knees before him
    b. spoke in tongues
    c. professed allegiance to the Risen Lord
    d. promised to follow the Mosaic Law

33. The followers of Christ were first known as Christians in:

a. Galilee   c. Iconium
b. Ephesus   d. Antioch

34. Herod was struck dead at Caesarea because he:

a. blasphemed   c. married his sister-in-law
b. persecuted the disciples   d. broke the Sabbath

35. When Paul and Barnabas returned to Jerusalem to defend their missionary work among the Gentiles, they were confronted by:

a. James   c. Pharisees
b. a mob   d. the original apostles

36. When Barnabus wanted to take John Mark with him and Paul on the second missionary journey, Paul objected because:

    a. he was too young
    b. he had deserted them once before

    c. he would be an extra burden on their
       hosts
    d. he was needed in Antioch

37. When the keeper of the prison at Phillipi discovered the doors to the prison open, he:

    a. fled with the released prisoners
    b. killed himself
    c. converted
    d. tried to recapture Paul

38. Gallio, the Roman proconsul of Achaia, refused to prosecute Paul because:

    a. he had secretly converted
    b. he would not intervene in a theological
       dispute
    c. he feared an insurrection
    d. the auguries warned him not to lay a
       hand on him

39. In Cenchrea, Paul made a vow and:

    a. swore never to eat meat
    b. shaved his head
    c. swore never to marry
    d. purified himself at the synagogue

40. The city of Ephesus was stirred up against Paul and his companions by the silversmiths because:

    a. Paul preached against idols
    b. the disputes between Christians and
       Jews were hurting business

    c. Paul tried to forbid work on the Sabbath

    d. Paul preached against usury

41. In Troas, a young Christian was killed when he:

    a. fell from a window

    b. preached the gospel in the marketplace

    c. tried to enter the synagogue

    d. was run over by a chariot

42. The prophet Agabus warned Paul not to reenter Jerusalem because:

    a. the Apostles would rule against him

    b. the Jews would arrest him

    c. the Romans would kill him

    d. the Pharisees would entrap him

43. Felix, the Roman governor, neither condemned Paul nor set him free, but kept him in Caesura for two years:

    a. out of fear the Jews would kill him

    b. while Paul's appeal was sent to Caesar

    c. out of hope that Paul would bribe him

    d. so that he could learn of this new doctrine

PAUL'S BEST LINES

The apostle was without doubt one of the greatest writers in all history. See how well you recall his most well-known statements by filling in the correct missing words:

44. It is more blessed to give than _____.

45. The wages of sin is _____.

46. Be not overcome of evil, but overcome evil _____.

47. It is better to marry than _____.

48. I am made all things to _____.

49. For now we see through a glass darkly, but then _____.

50. O death, where is _____?

51. God loveth a _____.

52. Let us not be weary in _____.

53. Labour of _____.

54. The day of the Lord so cometh as a _____ in the night.

55. We brought nothing into this world, and it is certain we can carry _____.

56. I have fought the _____.

57. I have kept _____.

REVELING IN REVELATION

58. John received his vision on the isle of Patmos:

    a. on the Lord's day
    b. from a whirlwind
    c. in a trance
    d. during the night in a dream

59. In his opening salutations to the seven churches, John praises their merits and names their faults. Which church does he condemn as being lukewarm?

a. Philadelphia   c. Laodicea
b. Pergamos   d. Thyatira

60. Around the throne of God, John saw four beasts. Which was *not* one of the beasts?

a. lion   c. calf
b. lamb   d. eagle

ARMAGEDDON

Revelation 16:16 names it as the site of the final battle between good and evil. From the Hebrew *har-megiddon* (mount of Megiddo), it can be located at a critically important pass through the lower foothills of Mount Carmel. Guarded by the fortress city of Megiddo, it is one of the bloodiest battle sites in world history—continuing to this day. In biblical history alone it is the scene of victories by Deborah and later Gideon, as well as the fatal defeats of Saul and later Josiah.

61. No man on earth or in heaven was worthy to open the Book with Seven Seals but only:

    a. Him that sat upon the throne
    b. the Lamb with seven horns and seven eyes
    c. the elders
    d. the angel

62. As the first four seals were broken, out of the Book came:

    a. horsemen
    b. earthquakes
    c. the names of the saints
    d. the hundred and forty-four thousand of Israel

63. Before the seventh trumpet was sounded, evil was temporarily victorious when it triumphs over:

    a. the angels' army of two hundred thousand thousand
    b. the great cities of the earth
    c. two witnesses
    d. the four beasts

64. At the sounding of the seventh trumpet, John saw "a great wonder in heaven," which was:

    a. a great red dragon
    b. a woman clothed in the sun
    c. fire and brimstone descending on the earth
    d. the glory of the Lord

65. The number of the beast out of the earth is:

    a. 666
    b. 777
    c. 1,260
    d. 42

66. The 144,000 who stood with the Lamb on Mount Sion were distinguished by the fact that they were:

    a. martyrs
    b. saints
    c. repentant sinners
    d. virgins

67. Upon the forehead of the woman arrayed in purple and scarlet sitting upon a scarlet covered beast was the name:

    a. Babylon
    b. Egypt
    c. Jezebel
    d. Temptress

68. John foresaw the wife of the Lamb "arrayed in fine linen, clean and white: for the fine linen is the righteousness of the saint." This wife of the Lamb was:

    a. the Church
    b. Israel
    c. Jerusalem
    d. The Queen of Heaven

Answers to CHAPTER 1:

"HOW WELL DO YOU KNOW THE GOOD BOOK?"

≈≈≈

page 17

1. (b) **Sarah,** with 56 mentions. Rachel is second with 47 mentions. The Virgin Mary is mentioned or referred to only 19 times. Eve, the mother of the entire human race, is mentioned by name only 4 times, and 2 of those are in the New Testament.

2. (a) **David,** with 1,085 mentions. Moses is second with 740 mentions.

3. (d) **Psalms** is the longest book, with 2,461 verses in 150 chapters.

4. (a) The **Second Epistle of John** contains just 13 verses.

5. **"Jesus wept"** (John 11:35). It occurs when Jesus sees the sepulcher in which Lazarus has been laid.

6. **"Lord, save me"** (Matthew 14:30) is Peter's prayer when he begins to sink after trying to walk on water.

7. (b) **Isaiah** is quoted or referred to 419 times in 23 New Testament books. Psalms follows closely with 414 citations.

8. (d) **Revelation** quotes or refers to passages from 32 books of the Old Testament.

9. (a) The **Book of Jasher** is referred to twice, once in Joshua 10:13 and again in 2 Samuel 1:18. The Book of Zephaniah is included among the Prophetic Books, while Baruch and Judith are Apocryphal books. Other books, presum-

ably lost, mentioned in the Old Testament are the Book of Wars; the Chronicles of David, the Book of Gad, the Book of the Prophet Iddo, the Book of Nathan, and the Book of Jehu.

10. (d) **Daniel** is not regarded as a Prophetic Book in the Hebrew Bible, where it is included with the Writings. Its use of a setting in the Babylonian Captivity and its attribution to a prophet named Daniel are thought to have been a coded way of writing about the persecutions which took place some four hundred years later under Antiochus Epiphanes.

11. (d) **Twelve.**

12. (b) **Jeremiah.**

13. **Esther.**

14. (c) The apostate king **Manasseh** ascended to the throne at the age of twelve and reigned over Judah for fifty-five years (2 Kings 21:1).

15. (d) **Zimri** was king of Israel for just seven days before a rebellion forced him to commit suicide (I Kings 16:15–20).

16. **Genesis** and the **Gospel According to John.**

17. **Psalms** is a collection of five books, which is why some psalms are repeated or rendered more than once with only slight changes.

18. (a) The most common noun, by far, is **Lord**—which is used 7,836 times. *Israel* is used only 2,586 times and *God* only 4,447 times. The common word *water* is used only 376 times.

19. (a) **Judges** is considered the oldest book of the Bible, and linguistic analysis—the latest technique of biblical scholarship—shows it has suffered the least amount of tampering or revision of any of the ancient texts.

20. (d) Many students of the Bible—including Eusebius, Jerome, Erasmus, Luther, and Calvin, to name only a few —have doubted that the **Second Epistle of Peter** was written by the apostle, and dates have been assigned as late as A.D. 125. It was not unusual for letters or entire books to be ascribed to a famous person or written in someone else's name.

21. (b) **Moses.**

22. The main characters of the eponymous **Ruth** and **Job** are, respectively, a Moabess and "a man in the land of Uz," i.e., an Edomite.

23. **Paul** is the author of thirteen Epistles, each of which is a book of the Bible.

24. **Genesis.**

25. The last word in the Bible is **Amen.**

Answers to CHAPTER **2**:

"THE PENTATEUCH"

≈≈≈

page 25

MEMORABLE COMMENTS

1. Reading: Genesis 3
Answer: (c) God means Adam literally *is* dust (Gen 3:19) since it was only a little while before that he "formed man of the dust of the ground, and breathed into his nostrils the breath of life; and man became a living soul" (Gen 2:7). In the

Roman Catholic and Anglican traditions, this curse of original sin is recalled on Ash Wednesday in the solemn injunction, "Remember, man, that **thou art dust and unto dust thou shalt return.**"

2. Reading: Genesis 4
Answer: (c) **"Am I my brother's keeper?"** (Gen 4:9) is a question unlikely ever to be resolved, although the criminality of its first asker may tip the scales in favor of a positive rather than a negative reply.

3. Reading: Genesis 45
Answer: (b) Although there are still some people who manage to live off **"the fat of the land"** (Gen 45:18), it's a little harder to do today.

4. Reading: Exodus 2
Answer: (b) When Moses' wife, Zipporah, bore him a son, he named him Gershom, which in Hebrew means "stranger there," for he said, "**I am a stranger in a strange land**" (Gen 2:22). Moses' sense of alienation in a foreign country presaged the Diaspora of the Jews, in which they became strangers in nations throughout the world.

5. Reading: Exodus 5–15
Answer: (c) **"Let my people go,"** demanded Moses nine times. God told Moses beforehand that he would "harden" Pharaoh's heart (Exod 4:21). So in rejecting Moses' plea, Pharaoh was unconsciously acting out the will of God. But why would God have wanted Pharaoh to reject what he had sent Moses to demand? It's been suggested that God wanted Israel to go through an experience that created a new history. He also wanted to impress on them, through the plagues and the miracles, the power and majesty of the God who was liberating them, so that the new history would be God-centered.

6. Reading: Numbers 22–24
Answer: (a) It may be that Balaam exclaimed **"what hath God wrought!"** (Num 23:23) out of amazement less at

Israel's size than at his own inability to deliver the curse for which King Balak was so obviously willing to pay. (In literature a "Balaam's curse" turns out as a blessing.) The story makes great fun of this soothsayer-for-hire whose own donkey had better foresight than he did, since at least the donkey saw the angel with the flaming sword standing in the middle of the road.

FAMOUS PEOPLE

7. Reading: Genesis 4–6
Answer: (b) **Cain** and his offspring do not merit a place in the great genealogy which will extend from his brother Seth through the saintly Enoch (who "walked with God") to Noah and thus to the rest of the human race.

8. Reading: Genesis 4
Answer: (b) A man bearing the "mark of Cain" meant in medieval times and afterward a murderer, but God placed the original mark on Cain to **protect** him.

9. Answers (from Genesis): Noah: g (8:20), h (9:21); Abel: c (4:2); Cain: a (5:17), d (4:2); Nimrod: b (10:9); Shechem: p (34:2); Abraham: k (20:7), m (18:13); Rachel: e (29:9); Lamech: i (4:23); Melchezidek: f (14:18); Naamah: j (4:22); Tubalcain: l (4:22); Lot: n (19:33) but also possibly Cain with a sister (4:17); Enoch: o (5:24).

10. Reading: Genesis 18
Answer: (c) She **laughed.** This very human interchange concludes with Sarah denying that she laughed and God replying, somewhat petulantly, "Oh, yes you did" (18:15).

11. Reading: Genesis 32
Answer: (c) In a time before written wills, the legal heir was designated by being granted custodianship of the **household gods.** By stealing them, Rachel was claiming the inheritance for her husband, Jacob, against her brothers.

12. Reading: Genesis 32

Answer: (d) Jacob had safely gotten his family across the river and sent his goods ahead with the servants. Then in the most direct and primitive language in the Old Testament "there **wrestled a man** with him until the breaking of the day" (32:24).

Notice how the identity of the assailant unfolds. At first it is "a man." Is it Esau? Or one of his agents sent to assassinate Jacob? As the struggle wears on, the rival is revealed to have strength he seems not to be using, for he wounds Jacob by only "touching the hollow of his thigh." Is it an angel? It is a power, Jacob decides, capable of giving a blessing, and Jacob will not let him go until he does. "What is thy name?" Jacob is asked and, when he gives it, is told: "Thy name shall be called no more Jacob, but Israel: for as a prince hast thou power with God and men, and hast prevailed." It is only after dawn, when he is alone, that Jacob is convinced of the experience he has just endured and says to himself, "I have seen God face to face, and my life is preserved." Having been renamed himself, he renames the place Peniel—*God's Face*.

What does this story mean? The author Reynolds Price notes that it is too simply rendered to be metaphor. It is stripped as bare as any story can be, as simply told as any story told by a father or grandfather determined to engrave a memory in the minds of his offspring and to have them pass it on. It says plainly, *This was not a dream, this happened to me.* In other words, it seems to mean exactly what it says: God descended on his Chosen One at the very moment of the man's greatest weakness, wrestled with him, afflicted him with a mark as a sign to his sons, bestowed on him a new name, blessed him, and left him grateful and strengthened for the trials ahead.

13. Reading: Genesis 29

Answer: (b) This is the first recorded instance of bait-and-switch. After working seven years to gain Rachel's hand, Jacob apparently drank too much at his wedding feast and found himself in the morning married instead to **Leah** (Gen 29:23–25). But love conquers all, and Jacob agreed—we don't know how readily—to serve another seven years to win his true bride.

14.I. *Abraham played the same trick on Pharaoh* (h) *and Abimelech* (d) (Gen 12:11–20; 20). Afraid that her great beauty would cause Pharaoh to kill him in order to claim Sarah for his own, Abraham passed her off as his sister. Pharaoh promptly took her into his household as a concubine and rewarded Abraham with sheep, oxen, camels, and slaves. To Pharaoh's credit, as soon as pestilence in the land made him aware of the deception, he upbraided Abraham, gave Sarah back to him, and threw him out of the country. Without any hint of embarrassment, Genesis (13:2) lets us know that as a result Abraham was "very rich." Either in a scriptural doublet or because it worked so well the first time, in chapter 20 Abraham pulled the same stunt on King Abimelech of Gerar. This time God warned the king in time for him to avoid sleeping with Sarah so that his land was saved. But the king rewarded Abraham with a thousand pieces of silver anyway. (In what may be a scriptural triplet, the same story is told of Isaac and "Abimelech, king of the Philistines" in chapter 26.)

II. *Jacob fooled Isaac* (f) (Gen 27). Esau, the firstborn son, married two local Hittite women, much to the displeasure of his mother, Rebecca. When it came time for the blessing to be handed down, she abetted Jacob in deceiving his father. In an earlier incident (25: 29–34), Esau had sold his inheritance to Jacob for a mess of pottage, but this seems a later invention designed to show that the inheritance really belonged to Jacob (it is, after all, the winners who write history); otherwise Esau's fury at being cheated out of the blessing doesn't make much sense.

In the ancient period, a father's oral blessing was both a religious and legal act, like a marriage vow.

III. *Rachel tricked Laban* (g) (Gen 31:33–35). When Laban caught up with the fleeing Jacob and his family, he immediately began a search for the household gods that were stolen. Rachel hid them under a camel's saddle and sat on it, telling her father she couldn't get up because "the custom of women is upon me." Laban was not the only father, before or since, to be embarrassed when confronted with his daughter's femaleness, and Rachel was not the only daughter to use it to her advantage.

IV. *Joseph tricked Benjamin* (b) (Gen 44: 2–13). Joseph

had his steward plant a silver cup on Benjamin so that he could have him arrested and held in Egypt. Joseph seemed torn: on the one hand reluctant to reveal who he was to his brothers, perhaps for fear of losing his position with Pharaoh, and on the other, unwilling to be separated again from his youngest brother, the only other son of his mother, Rachel. Only when Judah appealed to him, saying that Benjamin's disappearance would kill their father, was the impasse broken.

V. *Simeon and his brothers deceived Shechem* (a) *and his father* (Gen 34). Shechem was so enamored of Dinah, whom he had defiled, that he talked his countrymen into meeting the condition her brothers had laid down for marriage: circumcision. After three days, "when they were sore" and presumably not capable of mounting a defense, Simeon and his brother Levi entered their town and avenged their sister by slaughtering Shechem, his father, and every other male. For this impetuous act of violence, they with their older brother, Reuben (whose violation was to have slept with one of his father's concubines), would be passed over in favor of the fourth son, Judah (Gen 49:3–7).

VI. *Tamar deceived Judah* (e) (Gen 38). Interrupting the narrative of Joseph for no apparent reason, this self-contained story could easily be expanded into a two-hour docudrama. According to custom and, later, Law (Deut 25:5–6), it was Onan's responsibility to impregnate his dead brother's wife; the child then would continue the line of the firstborn and receive the inheritance of Judah. Onan, however, was having none of it. His act of *coitus interruptus* was an act of defiance against both the tradition and God's will, and he paid for it with his life. Years later when Judah seemed to be reneging on his promise to Tamar that she would marry the next in line, the youngest son, Shelah, she used deceit to insert herself back into the picture, playing the prostitute to bear heirs to Judah. It is evident that Tamar was a woman not to be tampered with, and even Judah admitted, "she has been more righteous than I" (Gen 38:26) as he acknowledged the legitimacy of her twin sons, Zarah and Pharez, from whom the royal line would descend (Matt 1:3).

15. Reading: Genesis 49
Answer: (d) **Judah.** Although the twelve sons of Jacob, including Joseph, would found the tribes of Israel, it was Judah who received the Covenant blessing (Gen 49: 8–12) and from whose line would come David and the Anointed One, "the Lion of the tribe of Juda, the Root of David" (Rev 5:5).

The reader may ask why these questions of genealogy are so important. To Old Testament Jews and to the early Christians, nothing could be more important. David's legitimacy, the legitimacy of his line, and therefore the legitimacy of the nation of Israel came from his claim to Jacob's prophetic blessing of Judah. Likewise, the Davidic descent of Jesus assured his legitimacy because it fulfilled the prophecies that the Messiah would come from the royal line: "There shall come forth a rod out of the stem of Jesse, and a Branch shall grow out of his roots: And the Spirit of the Lord shall rest upon him, the spirit of wisdom and understanding, the spirit of counsel and might, the spirit of knowledge and of the fear of the Lord" (Isa 1:1–2).

This accounts for the detailed attention Matthew gives in the New Testament to the genealogy of Joseph. But what difference does Joseph's lineage make since Joseph was not the biological father of Jesus? The modern idea that paternity is genetic was unknown to the ancients. To them paternity was a legal institution (perhaps, in fact, the first legal institution), not a biological fact, and therefore the adoptive father was the real father whether or not he physically conceived of the child. Therefore, the lineage of Jesus was the lineage of Joseph. (This was by no means unique to the Jews. Adoption was common in the Roman aristocratic families as a means of continuing the line. Blood relationships had nothing to do with it; money often did, with the adoptee paying handsomely for the privilege of being adopted.) Joseph's role in the Messianic drama was to take the unborn son of Mary under his wing and to adopt him into the royal line; this point was implicit when the angel first addressed him as "Joseph, thou son of David" (Matt 1:20).

16. Reading: Genesis 11, 25, 29, 38
Answer: (c) **Tamar** was not barren. Sarah (11:30),

Rebekah (25:21), and Rachel (29:31) were, perhaps as a sign to Abraham and his descendents that in each generation their family, and by extension the Hebrew nation that sprang from it, was dependent on God's caring intervention.

17. Reading: Exodus 34
Answer: (c) ". . . for the Lord, whose name is **Jealous,** is a jealous God" (Exod 34:14).

18. Reading: Genesis 14, 19, 20; Exodus 18
Answer: (d) **Bera,** king of Sodom, can only be inferred to have been an atheist from the evil practices of his people. Melchizedek (14:18) was "the priest of the most high God" who offered bread and wine and blessed Abraham. Abimelech, king of the Philistines (20:1–18), showed himself to be God-fearing in his reaction to his discovery that Sarah was Abraham's wife. Jethro, the father-in-law of Moses, was "the priest of Midian" and offered a sacrifice of thanksgiving for the delivery of the Israelites (Exod 18:1–12). In fact, almost everyone named in the Pentateuch, Hebrew or Gentile, friend or foe, seemed to believe in the one transcendent God. When "gods" are mentioned at all, it is only to contrast their weakness to the power of the one true God.

Scholarly opinion in the nineteenth century was nearly unanimous in regarding monotheism as an evolutionary development from polytheism. Opinion is much more divided now, with many scholars believing polytheism is a corruption of an original monotheism, as demonstrated by the fact that most primitive cultures had a concept of the "Great Spirit" or "Great God." The Bible seems to testify to monotheism as the original religious impulse.

The Gentile priest Melchizedek will become an immensely important figure in later history. Psalm 110 extols him as priest preceding, and therefore superior to, the priests of Israel, and since he was "king of Salem" or Jerusalem, claims for the king of Jerusalem and therefore to the Davidic line the role of priest-king. The Letter to the Hebrews picks up this line of reasoning, and the fact that he offered bread and wine, to present him as the prefiguration of the priesthood of Christ, who was not born of the Levite or priestly line of Israel but of the Davidic or royal line. The Orthodox, Catholic, and Anglican churches continue this tradition by consecrating their priests into "the order of Melchizedek" (Ps 110:4).

19. Reading: Deuteronomy 34
Answer: (b) **God.** The answer rests on a pronoun. The passage in the King James Version reads, "So Moses the servant of the LORD died there in the land of Moab, according to the word of the LORD. And he buried him . . ." (Deut 34:6). The New International Version, the Jerusalem Bible, and The Revised Standard Version retain the same ambiguity. The New English Bible is neutral on the point: "And he was buried . . ." The Bible in Today's English is positive: "The LORD buried him . . ." The next sentence tells us that no man knows where he was buried, which supports the idea that God dealt with this matter himself.

WHAT AND WHY

20. Reading: Genesis 3
Answer: (b) **The woman gave him the fruit.** Adam's reasoning seems to be that since God created woman, it's his fault (Gen 3:12). And if not God's, then the woman's.

21. Reading: Genesis 4
Answer: (b) Cain murdered Abel because **he was jealous when God chose Abel's sacrifice over his.** But perhaps God rejected his sacrifice because the thought was already in his mind: "sin lieth at the door," God warned him (Gen 4:7). The Revised Standard Version is clearer: ". . . sin is lurking at the door; its desire is for you, but you must master it."

22. Reading: Genesis 17
Answer: (d) Circumcision was an outward sign of the Hebrews' right to the land of Canaan. The origins of circumcision as a religious rite are unknown, but it was practiced in prehistoric times by the Egyptians, Moabites, Arabs, and other Western Semites. It may have been related to fertility cults; indeed after telling Abraham to **circumcise himself and all his**

meñ and all male children thereafter, the Lord announced that
Abraham and Sarah would have a son. It could also have been
a primitive hygienic practice. Or it could have been a sacrificial
act in contrast to the pagan practice of child sacrifice which so
horrified the later prophets. At the Council of Jerusalem in A.D.
50 Peter and the apostles ruled that circumcision was not to be
a requirement for Christian converts, on the grounds that the
new covenant had now superseded the old.

23. Reading: Genesis 18–19
    Answer: (b) Abraham tried to save Sodom by asking
God if he intended to destroy the righteous with the wicked.
After some judicious bargaining, he extracted from God the
agreement that he would not destroy the city if ten righteous
men could be found there. Now apparently God had gone him
one better, for the angel clearly was under instructions (Gen
19:22) **not to destroy Sodom as long as Lot—the only righteous man in the place—remained.**

24. Reading: Genesis 19
    Answer: (d) Although Jewish legend has it that the
towns of Sodom and Gomorrah were greedy, and we can see
from the text that the inhabitants planned homosexual rape
against the angels, the major sin seems to have been **inhospitality.** In a nomadic society, where settlements were often few
and far between, the obligations of hospitality were strict: It
was a solemn duty to feed, clothe, and house strangers. Lot felt
so bound by this rule that he was willing to sacrifice his two
daughters to the mob in order to protect the strangers who had
come "under the shadow of my roof" (Gen 19:8). But the custom of Sodom seemed to have been to assault and rob strangers, and for this crime it and its sister city were destroyed.

25. Reading: Genesis 21
    Answer: (a) "Whereupon she said unto Abraham,
'Cast out this bondswoman and her son: for the son of this
bondswoman **shall not be heir with my son, even with
Isaac'** " (Gen 21:10). Abraham grieved over this, but the Lord
told him not to: "I will make of him a great nation" (Gen
21:18). But this casting out was not the last of Ishmael in Gene-

sis. When Abraham died, he showed up again at the burial: "And his sons Isaac and Ishmael buried him . . ." (Gen 25:9). None of Abraham's other sons are mentioned. Does this imply a kind of legitimacy for Ishmael or a reconciliation? The fact that his generations are given and his death is recorded (Gen 25:12–18) is surely a sign of great respect. By tradition, Ishmael is the founder of the Arab race.

26. Reading: Genesis 39
Answer: (a) Sexual harassment runs both ways, as this story of Joseph—imprisoned because **Potiphar's wife accused him of rape**—reminds us.

27. Reading: Exodus 4
Answer: (a) **He had not circumcised his son.** This is a puzzling incident. It is not explained how Moses, by upbringing an Egyptian, and Zipporah, a Midianite, were supposed to know that their son should have been circumcised, but Zipporah didn't waste a moment in setting matters right (Gen 4:24–26). But why did God, having gone to so much trouble to recruit Moses, to overcome his doubts, and to imbue him with a sense of his destiny, suddenly try to kill him?

28. Reading: Exodus 7–11
Answer: (c) The ten plagues were the Nile's water turned to blood, overrunning of frogs, infestation of lice, swarms of flies, disease for the livestock, boils and sores, hail destroyed the crops, three days of thick darkness, and the death of the firstborn. There was no **infestation of ants.**

29. Reading: Exodus 16
Answer: (d) The Biblical account of **manna,** "a small round thing, as small as hoarfrost on the ground . . . like coriander seed, white, and the taste of it was like wafers made of honey" (Exod 16:14, 31) is correct in every detail. Manna has been found by modern botanists to be the secretion of a plant louse that infests tamarisk trees indigenous to the Sinai desert. The remarkable accuracy of the description would seem to confirm a Mosaic dating for the original version of this account. By the way, in Hebrew, *manna* means "what is it?"—

which would have been a natural enough question for the Hebrews to ask.

30. Reading: Exodus 24
Answer: (b) When **the elders of Israel broke bread on Mt. Sinai,** they were allowed to see God, even stare at him for an entire afternoon. Yet the only descriptive detail is that "there was under his feet a paved work of sapphire stone, and as it were the body of heaven in his clearness" (Exod 24:10). Not a word was spoken.

31. Reading: Exodus 31
Answer: (c) Moses was given "two tables of testimony, tables of stone, written with **the finger of God**" (Exod 31:18). By the way, the word "write" first appears in the Bible in Exodus 17:14, when Moses is told to "write this for a memorial in a book and rehearse it in the ears of Joshua . . ." This would seem to be the injunction for the creation of the Old Testament.

32. Reading: Exodus 20
Answer: (a) **"Thou shalt love thy neighbor as thyself"** is the second of Jesus' two great summaries of the commandments (Matt 22:39), not one of the Ten Commandments. It is a quote from Leviticus 19:18. (The first is, "Thou shalt love the Lord thy God with all thy heart, and with all thy soul, and with all thy mind.")

33. Reading: Exodus 23; Numbers 28–29
Answer: (d) **Hanukkah,** or the Feast of Lights, was established after the overthrow of the tyranny of Antiochus Epiphanes and restoration of worship in the Temple in Jerusalem about 167 B.C. (1 Macc 4:56).

Answers to CHAPTER **3**:

"THE HISTORICAL BOOKS"

≈≈≈

page 40

MEMORABLE COMMENTS

1. Reading: Judges 1–2
Answer: (c) When it became clear that the tribes couldn't clear out all the Canaanite inhabitants, the Lord said ". . . I will not drive them out from before you; but they shall be as **thorns in your sides,** and their gods shall be a snare unto you" (2:3). As the ensuing books will show, truer words were never spoken.

2. Reading: Ruth 1
Answer: (c) As anyone who has ever attended a wedding where this passage is read will know, Ruth said to Naomi, ". . . **wither thou goest I will go;** and where thou lodgest, I will lodge: thy people shall be my people, and thy God my God: Where thou dies, will I die, and there will I be buried: the LORD do so to me, and more also, if ought but death part thee and me" (1:16–17). Ruth was a Moabite, and by this declaration converted to Judaism. Her devotion and loyalty were rewarded by the God whom she adopted as her own.

3. Reading: 1 Samuel 9–12
Answer: (a) "And all the people shouted, and said, **'God save the king'** " (10:24). A minor point: Every translation after the King James Version renders the Hebrew as "Long live

the king." Were the English translators of the seventeenth century giving a favorite English slogan an ancient Biblical lineage? The British national anthem, "God Save the King," was written at about the same time the King James Version was translated.

Note in the reading that Saul protests his selection by Samuel, saying, "Am I not a Benjamite, of the smallest of the tribes of Israel? and my family the least of all the families of the tribe of Benjamin?" (9:21). The Benjamites were closely allied with the Ephraimites, the most powerful tribe. Only two of the children of Jacob were born to his beloved Rachel, Benjamin and Joseph. The families of Joseph's two sons, Ephraim and Manneseh, were accorded tribal status by the time the Hebrews entered the Promised Land, because they were so populous. These three tribes were known because of their lineage as the "Rachel tribes" and were closely connected by intermarriage and geography, having settled the northern territory. Most of the judges had come from the Ephraimites. The selection of a Benjamite as first king might have been a way to placate Ephraimite feeling without extending Ephraimite power.

4. Reading: 1 Samuel 13–15

Answer: (c) And Samuel made it very clear that this man "after his own heart" would not be the disobedient Saul but a newly chosen instrument of divine will. When God sent Samuel to find a new king, the prophet identified David, the youngest son of Jesse, of the tribe of Judah, in Bethlehem.

5. Reading: 1 Samuel: 27–31; 2 Samuel: 1–2

Answer: (c) In the "Song of the Bow" (2 Sam 1:19–27), which David ordered to be taught to all the children of Judah, David showed the magnanimity of his spirit as he lamented the death of his enemy Saul and of his beloved friend—and rival for the throne—Jonathan. "How are the mighty fallen!" he exclaimed, and of Jonathan he said, "Thy love to me was wonderful, passing the love of women." The title of the song may have come from a favorite nickname for Jonathan: he had once used his archery to signal to David that his life was in danger (1 Sam 20–21).

6. Reading: 2 Kings 2

Answer: (a) When Isaiah told Hezekiah "**to set thine house in order,**" he was giving advice likely to be heard today from a doctor to the patient with an incurable disease. In Hezekiah's case, the Lord relented and allowed him to live for fifteen more years.

FAMOUS PEOPLE

7. Reading: Joshua 2, 6

Answer: (c) **Rahab's** courage in protecting Joshua's spies must have been inspiring to the invading Hebrews. In appreciation of her heroism, Joshua ordered that she and her kinsmen be saved before Jericho was burned to the ground (6:22–23). Rahab, a prostitute, was later married to a member of the tribe of Judah, became the mother of Boaz, who married Ruth; and with Tamar and Ruth is one of the three women listed by name in the genealogy of Jesus (Matt 1:5).

8. Reading: Judges 4–5

Answer: (c) Jael fulfilled Deborah's prophecy that Sisera would die at "the hand of a woman" (4:9). This may have been a rebuke to Barak, war leader of the Israelites, who wouldn't go into battle without Deborah's presence. It was certainly an insult to Sisera to die at the hands of a woman rather than in battle, but then again, he was the one who ran away. For her action, Jael is praised in the "Song of Deborah" as "blessed over women."

9. Reading: Judges 6–8

Answer: (b) The Lord chose Gideon, "a mighty man of valor," to fight off the Midianites even though Gideon protested that "my family is poor in Manasseh and I am the least in my father's house." After assurances that the Lord would be with him, he destroyed the altar of Baal at night, and then seemed to have very large second thoughts: What if the Lord really wasn't with him? So he devised a test with **a piece of fleece** (6: 36–40): if in the morning it had dew on it and the earth beside it was dry, then he'd know the Lord was with him. When that happened, it seemed to dawn on Gideon that it could have been an accident, so the next night he asked that the fleece be dry and the ground wet, and when it happened, he stepped forward with new confidence to lead the people.

Note after his first successes how Gideon had to mollify the men of Ephraim, since he came from the related but minor Rachel tribe of Manasseh (8:1–3).

10. Reading: Judges 11–12

Answer: (a) When Jephthah vowed to **sacrifice "whatsoever cometh out of the doors of my house to meet me,"** what could he have been thinking of? A sheep? The family dog? He only had one daughter, and sure enough, she "came out to meet him with timbrels and with dances . . ." (11:34). He seemed shocked—"he rent his clothes and said, Alas, my daughter!" Thus a "Jephthah's vow" came to mean a promise rashly given and later regretted.

This inexplicable story with its tragic ending has caused a lot of consternation, but this may entail a misunderstanding on the part of later generations of customs so familiar in Old Testament times that they required no detailed explanation. Medieval Talmudic commentators and modern Christian scholars, including Dr. Gleason Archer of Trinity Evangelical Divinity School, note several facts:

1. Human sacrifice is expressly forbidden in Leviticus (18:21; 20:2–5) and Deuteronomy (12:31; 18:10).

2. Jephthah's daughter was given two months not to bewail her coming death but to bewail her *virginity* (11:37–38).

3. After her mourning period, Jephthah "did with her according to his vow which he had vowed; and she knew no man" (11:39). That latter remark would be inane if she had been put to death.

4. "And it was a custom in Israel" (11:39) certainly does not refer to human sacrifice, which wasn't, but could lead us to the real answer: a life of consecrated service before the tabernacle. Jephthah's daughter, like Anna in the days of Jesus (Luke 2:36–37), was probably joining the women who served the tabernacle and to whom brief references are made in Exodus (38:8) and 1 Samuel (2:22). Jephthah was bemoaning the end of his line rather than the death of his daughter.

11. Reading: Judges 13–16

Answer: (a) "And the angel of the Lord appeared unto the woman and said unto her, Behold now, thou art barren, and bearest not: but **thou shalt conceive and bear a son**" (13:3). The announcement to Manoah, mother of Samson, was repeated almost verbatim in the announcement to Mary, mother of Jesus: "And, behold, thou shalt conceive in thy womb, and bring forth a son . . ." (Luke 1:31). Manoah was instructed not to drink wine or eat any unclean thing because her son would be a "Nazarite unto God from the womb" (13:5).

What we might consider to be a health warning is, in fact, an act of consecration. The word "Nazarite" means "one who is separate." Nazarites dedicated themselves to God by not drinking wine or strong drink, not cutting their hair, not having contact with the dead, and not eating unclean food (Num 6:3–7). Samson and Samuel are the only persons specifically named as Nazarites in the Bible, although John the Baptist may have been one, as may have been the women associated with the tabernacle.

It is interesting that Samson, the first and one of only two Nazarites named, went on to violate his vows with seemingly reckless abandon. As the Philistines migrated from the Aegean to settle the coastal area of Canaan, they assumed overlordship of the tribe of Dan and those of Judah who lived in the area. The Danite Samson constituted a kind of one-man resistance force, and "he smote them hip and thigh." In one famous encounter (15:15–18), he slew a thousand "with the jawbone of an ass," so he had plenty of contact with dead bodies. He participated in feasts where there must have been plenty of drinking. And of course, he allowed the enticing Delilah to have his hair cut off.

12. Reading: Ruth

Answer: (b) ". . . and she came softly, and **uncovered his feet, and laid her down**" (3:7). By lying at the feet of Boaz, Ruth humbled herself as one of his servants. When he awoke with a start, she asked him to "spread . . . thy skirt over thine handmaid; for thou art a near kinsman" (3:9), i.e., spread your wings over me and become my protector by marrying me according to the duty of a near kinsman. Which, after clearing up some complications, Boaz happily did.

This is a wonderful story of faithfulness and love, but for most Hebrews the most important word in it was the last one: *David*. Ruth and Boaz became the great-grandparents of David (4:21–22), and in that fact lies the moral of the story. In the post-exilic period, foreign marriages were forbidden. The tale of Ruth argued powerfully and poetically for ending the ban: it showed a foreigner could not only enter into the covenant but become an instrument for elevating it to new heights. In other words, if it hadn't been for this Moabite woman, there would have been no David. For Christians, the message was even more powerful. By including Ruth in the Messianic line, the story showed that the Messiah was not meant for Jews alone but for the whole world.

13. Reading: 1 Samuel 16–17
Answer: (a) When Saul sought a **harpist** to soothe his troubled spirit, his servant told of a son of Jesse who was "cunning in playing" (16:18). David was summoned to court, where he found favor and even became Saul's armorbearer, but when war resumed, he returned to help his father while his older brothers went off to fight. It was on a mission to bring them supplies that David heard the giant Goliath's boastful challenge to the Israelite army and, ashamed that no Israelite would punish his blasphemy, decided to do it himself.

This, by the way, was not David's last encounter with giants. In a later war with the Philistines (2 Sam 21: 15–22), he was almost killed by one, and four others are mentioned in connection with the battle. Some anthropologists speculate that Goliath and these other giants may have been from aborigine stock. Perhaps Genesis 6:1–4 refers to the same race when it notes cryptically that "there were giants in the earth in those days." In Numbers 13:33, the spies sent out by Moses to reconnoiter Canaan report: "And there we saw the giants, the sons of Anak, which come of the giants: and we were in our own sight as grasshoppers, and so we were in their sight."

14. Reading: 1 Samuel 31; 2 Samuel 1
Answer: (c) The young Amalekite embellished the

news of Saul's death that he brought to David by claiming to have assisted the king in his suicide. This proved to be a fatal mistake. David asked, "How wast thou not afraid to stretch forth thine hand to destroy the Lord's anointed?" (1:14) and promptly **ordered the messenger executed.** David, who himself had already been anointed by Samuel, had good reason not to countenance regicide.

15. Reading: 2 Samuel 6
Answer: (b) ". . . Michal Saul's daughter looked through a window, and saw king David leaping and dancing before the Lord; and **she despised him** in her heart." Neither here nor in Chronicles 15:29, where the same information is conveyed in almost identical words, is there necessarily a cause and effect between David's dancing and Michal's despising. The words seem to go much deeper than mere disapproval.

Michal, the second daughter of Saul, loved David when she was first wed to him (1 Sam 18:20), and she even risked her father's wrath by saving his life (1 Sam 19:11–17). But after David's flight from court, the king married Michal to someone else. David went on to marry Abigail and Ahinnoam (1 Sam 25:42–44). Years later, when David was secure on the throne of Judah, he wanted to establish a legal claim to the throne of Israel, and the best way to do that was to reclaim his marriage rights to Michal and thereby his membership in the house of Saul, Israel's king. So Michal was taken from her husband of many years and sent to David, and, the chronicler notes poignantly, "her husband went with her along weeping behind her . . ." (2 Sam 3: 16).

Thus David's joy when he brought the ark of the Covenant into Jerusalem—thereby uniting religion and government, as he had already united north and south, in his own new capital—contrasted sharply with Michal's bitterness at the success of the very ambitions to which her happiness had been sacrificed.

16. Reading: 2 Samuel 13–19
Answer: (b) The story of **Absalom**'s murder of his older brother Amnon and subsequent rebellion against his father is one of the great narratives in world literature. It also

gives a stark look into the problems of succession in a polyga-
mous monarchy.

Polygamy for a king like David had many virtues and
one great vice. It showed the king's virility and vitality in a
time heavily influenced by ancient pagan fertility cults; it produced many possible heirs in a time when infant mortality was
more common than infant survival; and it made room for
many possible dynastic alliances in a time when family relationships superseded all others. Its great flaw, of course, was
that it could produce too many sons. Regardless of the supposed rules of succession, the son with the decisiveness,
strength, and ruthlessness to strike first could almost always
succeed, which meant that succession almost always entailed a
civil war. Absolom's problem, of course, was that he struck too
early and then acted too cautiously, but even so, he came very
close.

17. Reading: 1 Kings 3
Answer: (d) And because Solomon asked for **an understanding heart** instead of a long life, or riches, or the death
of his enemies, God gave him wisdom "so that there was none
like thee before thee, neither after thee shall any arise like unto
thee," and he also gave him that for which he did not ask "so
that there shall not be any among the kings like unto thee all
thy days" (3:12–13).

18. Reading: 1 Kings 16 (29–34)-22
Answer: (a) Ahab didn't need **Jezebel** to be a thor-
oughly despicable character, but she did her part to help. Evil
as they were and powerful as they were, the royal couple remained intimidated by the prophets Miciah and Elijah, who in
the end brought Ahab to humble himself before the Lord
(21:27). That was not enough, however, to make him heed
Miciah instead of his own paid prophets when he prophesized
defeat in an upcoming battle with the Syrians; Ahab was
killed, and in fulfillment of Elijah's curse, dogs licked his
blood.

For all his evildoing, Ahab is recorded as a great
builder (22:39) and his "ivory house" (actually built of white
stone with an interior of inlaid ivory) has been excavated in

Samaria, along with a nearby storehouse containing 500 ivory pieces.

Jezebel was a strong and determined woman, and a loyal if misguided queen to Ahab, and there is nothing to justify the later use of her name as a synonym for prostitute. The usage derives from identification of prostitution with bold behavior and heavy makeup, and the final description of the queen in 2 Kings 9:30 as she prepared to meet her murderer, "And when Jehu was come to Jezreel, Jezebel heard of it; and she painted her face."

Ahab is mostly remembered today because of his namesake, the whaling captain of Melville's *Moby Dick*, who rails against God and dies by following a false rather than a true prophecy. When a character early in the book declares, "Ahab's above the common. . . . He's *Ahab*, boy; and Ahab of old, thou knowest, was a crowned King!"—he is quickly rebuked, "And a very vile one. When that wicked King was slain, the dogs, did they not lick his blood?"

WHAT AND WHY

19. Reading: Joshua 5
Answer: (b) While the Hebrews who came out of Egypt were **circumcised,** for some reason those born in the wilderness were not, perhaps out of disobedience. (This seems inexplicable, especially considering that Moses was almost killed for not circumcising his son by Zipporah.) However, Joshua immediately obeyed the command of the Lord, in effect disabling his entire army at a moment of vulnerability, as a sign of faith and an expression of readiness to fulfill the ancient covenant made with Abraham.

20. Reading: Judges 1
Answer: (b) The invading Hebrews were at a technological disadvantage. The Bronze Age was giving way to the Iron Age, and the Canaanites had learned to forge the new metal from the Hittites. The Hebrews' softer bronze weapons barely made a dent, so to speak, in the **iron chariots** of the enemy. The demoralizing effect of this discovery led ten tribes,

all except Judah and Simeon, to disobey the will of God by compromising with the indigenous peoples and settling in among them.

21. Reading: Judges 4

Answer: (c) Only five things are known about Deborah: She was a married woman, she was a prophetess, she was the sole judge of Israel at the time, she "dwelt **under the palm tree** of Deborah," and Barak, the Israelite war captain, would not go into battle unless she did. We can only deduce from this fragmentary information what a commanding personality she must have been. For one thing, unlike Sarah, Rebekah, Rachel, Tamar, and, later, Ruth and even Mary, she is one of the few prominent women in the entire Bible not in the Davidic and Messianic line, and unlike Esther, there is no doubt of her historicity. For another, she was the only woman of the thirteen judges who arose in Israel in the approximately 410 years before the monarchy. She was not a queen, but she ruled an extremely patriarchal and male-dominated society, and her rule was so complete that the army would not move without her. This was some woman.

22. Reading: Judges 9

Answer: (a) Abimelech decided to transform his father Gideon's fame into a permanent monarchy with himself as the heir and monarch. This first required that he murder all his half-brothers, who would naturally resist such a claim, which his mother's relatives in Sechem helped him do. Jotham escaped and laid out the curse of the trees. Like the people of Sechem, **the trees wanted a king,** but the really important trees refused, preferring to keep to the roles that God had created them to perform, the olive to make oil, the fig to make fruit, etc. The only tree that would accept was the most common and worthless, the bramble bush. Jotham asked, do you really want to be ruled by a bramble bush like Abimelech? Three years later, the answer was no. Abimelech was killed, and the rule of the judges returned.

23. Reading: Judges 14

Answer: (c) The **riddle** was, "Out of the eater came

forth meat [food], and out of the strong came forth sweetness"
(14:12). Try this on your next dinner guests and you'll find
them to be as perplexed as Samson's were. The plain fact is,
this riddle makes no sense unless one knows what the reader
of this chapter knows, that Samson killed a lion in whose car-
cass bees had made a hive and produced honey. Not wanting
to lose a substantial wager, the guests finally convinced Samson's wife, their kinswoman, to wring the answer out of him.
She succeeded with the same kind of remonstration that
proved effective for Delilah later, which shows how little Samson learned from his experiences. (In fact, he seemed remarkably dim.) In this instance, when the guests spring the correct
answer on him, he responded in one of history's memorable
pouts: "If ye had not plowed with my heifer, ye had not found
out my riddle" (14:18).

24. Reading: Judges 19–21
Answer: (b) The Levite passed by Jerusalem, which
was still held by the non-Israelite Jesubites, in order to spend
the night among his own countrymen in Gibeah, a Benjamite
city. An elderly Ephraimite in the city offered him hospitality,
but then—in a scene with strong overtones from Sodom—a
crowd gathered at the old man's house demanding the host
produce the Levite "that we may know him" (19:22—compare
Gen 19:5). As Lot offered his two daughters to the Sodomite
crowd, the old man offered his daughter and the Levite's concubine. The concubine was finally given over to the mob and
was raped and killed. Enraged (and perhaps a little guilty
about his own cowardice), the Levite **carved her body into
twelve pieces** and sent one to each of the tribes of Israel.

The Israelites punished the tribe of Benjamin with a
massacre which nearly wiped it out. Gibeah became a synonym for the atrocity which occurred there (see Hos 9:9) and a
symbol for Israel's sinfulness.

The whole sad period of Judges is summed up in its
last sentence, which follows this story: "In those days there
was no king in Israel: every man did that which was right in
his own eyes." To anyone who wonders, moral relativism has
been tried before.

25. Reading: 1 Samuel 1–3
Answer: (a) "The word of the Lord was precious in those days" (3:1). Eli the priest had raised wicked sons, symbolic of Israel's raising up of wicked children, causing the Lord to cut off his prophetic powers. In Eli's place he raised up "a faithful priest" (2:35), Samuel, consecrated from birth into the Nazarite vows and given as an apprentice into Eli's service. But Eli was apparently a good and wise man, and when **Samuel heard the voice of the Lord and mistook it for Eli's,** the old man knew what was happening and gently guided Samuel into the understanding of his prophetic gift. And when Samuel told Eli what the Lord had told him (about the destruction of Eli's line), Eli said, "It is the Lord: let him do what seemeth him good."

26. Reading: 1 Samuel 28
Answer: (b) Here is the famous Witch of Endor—in a passage Lord Byron called "the finest and most finished witch-scene that ever was written or conceived . . . it beats all the ghost stories I have ever read." A dark night, disguises, "gods ascending out the earth," cries, a flash of recognition, the old man "covered with a mantle," a fatal curse: this is the stuff of high drama.

The woman "**with a familiar spirit**" had evaded the king's order expelling sorcerers from the country and, when first approached, thought she was the victim of a sting. After receiving assurances that no harm would come to her, she acceded to Saul's request and called up the spirit of Samuel. When—to her amazement—Samuel actually appeared, he prophesied Saul's defeat at the hands of the Philistines and told him the Lord had said "tomorrow shalt thou and thy sons be with me" (28:19). This was a devastating blow to the already demoralized Saul.

The questions raised by this passage over the centuries have been countless. How could a witch call up a prophet? Does it mean that witchcraft is real? Was it Samuel or the devil that was raised up? If it was the devil, how could it deliver a true prophecy in God's name? The woman's own surprise at Samuel's apparition seems to answer many of these questions. She seemed totally caught off-guard and more than a little frightened. If we think of her more as a modern-day medium of the crystal ball and tarot card variety and less as a witch (which she is not called anywhere in the text), her surprise may be seen to spring from her success: maybe nothing like this had ever happened to her before. God used Saul's slippage into superstition as a final occasion to tell him why he had fallen from favor—and the woman did indeed become the medium for the message.

27. Reading: 2 Samuel 5
Answer: (a) **Jerusalem,** situated in the middle of the country, was even at that time still controlled by the Jesubites, a non-Hebrew tribe. It was well fortified, well situated, and—best of all for David's purposes not associated with either the northern or the southern tribes. David conquered it by capturing the mountain fortress of Zion around which the city was built and which became the center of the "city of David."

28. Reading: 2 Samuel 11–12
Answer: (a) David seemed desperate to cover up his adulterous act. When Bathsheba sent word **she was pregnant,** he immediately summoned her husband back from the front, in the hope he would sleep with his wife and think the child was his own. But Uriah had taken an oath not to enjoy the comforts of home while his comrades were in the field. David tried again, this time getting Uriah drunk, but again Uriah stuck to his oath. Finally, David instructed Joab his general to make sure Uriah was killed in battle, and when Bathsheba's mourning period was over, he married her.

All might have gone well after that, with only David and Joab knowing the secret, except that Nathan the prophet saw through the deception. He denounced the murder of Uriah to David's face and pronounced God's curse: "The sword will never depart from thine house" (12, 10). As the first consequence of the curse, and in spite of David's fervent prayers, his child by Bathsheba died.

There are a few minor points and one large one to be made about this story.

What was David doing at home anyway? It was the time of year "when kings go forth to battle" and the army was duly sent out to battle the Ammonites, but the nation's top military strategist "tarried in Jerusalem" (11:1). The chronicler's disapproval is obvious in this first verse. Perhaps success had gone to David's head. Perhaps he had grown contented and self-satisfied. But why would an absolute monarch resort to murder to cover up adultery? David was wise enough to know the gravity of one offense against the other. As commander in chief, was David subject to the same oath as Uriah? Was his real fear that his troops in the field would discover how their king was disporting himself at home while they suffered and bled? Whatever the reasons, the story makes clear the result.

One biblical commentator says, "We wish the life of David could have ended before Chapter 11 was written. The golden era has passed away and what is left is a checkered tale of sin and punishment." This is pious nonsense, which brings up a larger point. David was only a hero, and heroes aren't perfect; even saints aren't perfect. But David was a good enough man to accept Nathan's upbraiding and God's judgment. He confessed his sin and had his confession published (Psalm 51). He accepted the consequences. He remained loyal to God. He remained an instrument of God's will, a "man after mine own heart."

The sin was David's; nowhere is Bathsheba's complicity in her husband's murder suggested. From the tragedy came glory; from Bathsheba's union with David would come the king who would build the Temple and produce a golden age. In fact, it was the prophet Nathan himself who approached Bathsheba and guided her in helping Solomon ascend to the throne (1 Kgs 1:11). Perhaps as a prophet Nathan saw with his foresight what our commentator can't see in hindsight, that God will use the act of two imperfect people to glorify the house into which will be born Perfection itself.

29. Reading: 1 Kings 1, 2

Answer: (d) In his first act as king, the nineteen-year-old Solomon showed himself wiser in statecraft than his mother. Bathsheba had come to him with a seemingly innocuous request from Adonijah that he be allowed to marry Abishag the Shunammite. The new king immediately **ordered his brother put to death.**

Abishag was the beautiful young virgin selected for David in his old age when his servants grew alarmed at his weakened condition. She "cherished the king and ministered to him" even though "the king knew her not." Her devotion and service to the great hero king may have earned Abishag a popular following of her own. Her service would make her the only one to be in the old king's presence night and day; therefore she may have wielded power in the twilight of his monarchy by the simple but effective device of deciding who could enter into his chambers and who couldn't. The mention of Abishag's presence when Bathsheba asked the king to name Solomon as his heir (1:15) may hint at her importance by implying her endorsement—she, after all, would have been the one to let Bathsheba see David. After David's death, his widowed virgin queen would certainly have carried great prestige. No doubt Abonijah saw marriage to her as a way of enhancing his own status. Unfortunately for him, the wise Solomon saw things exactly the same way.

We don't know what happened to Abishag after she played her transitional role in this critical moment for the royal house. She is never mentioned again. However, since Solomon had seven hundred wives and three hundred concubines (1 Kgs 11:3), it's safe to assume that Abishag was among them.

30. Reading: 1 Kings

Answer: (c) Long thought to be merely legendary, Sheba is emerging from recent archeological discoveries as an important political and cultural center in the centuries after 1000 B.C., in what is modern Yemen. It seems to have controlled the strait between Arabia and Ethiopia that connects the Red Sea and the Gulf of Aden. (Recent sonic tests done by oil companies in this region have found large cities buried underneath the desert sand.) No doubt the "hard questions" the Queen wanted to prove Solomon with had as much to do with trade as with religion. The two seem to have gotten along, and the account in 1 Kings lists the gifts they exchanged. According to legend, they exchanged more than gifts: the emperors of Ethiopia long claimed descent from their union; the royal house was named "the Solomonid line," and one of the most ancient titles of the Ethiopian emperor, last applied to Halle Selassie, was "Lion of Judah."

The account of gifts, by the way, states that the gold of Ophir (10:11) came from Sheba, which implies that this was a very wealthy kingdom. In its day, "the gold of Ophir" was as famous as "the cedars of Lebanon" and "the balm of Gilead."

31. Reading: 2 Kings 1

Answer: (a) This Canaanite **god of Ekron** on whom a king of Israel relied more than the Lord became a synonym for Satan. It is easy to see how. In what may be one of the few puns in the entire Bible, a letter may have been intentionally changed in this verse to transform Baal-*zebul*, "lord of the Temple," and the probable title of this local deity, into Baal-*zebub*, "lord of the flies," i.e., ruler over death and decay. By the time of Jesus, the name had further been corrupted into Beelzebub (Matt 10:25), and his identification with Satan as either a prince of darkness or the fallen angel himself was complete.

32. Reading: 1 Kings 19

Answer: (c) "And he said, Go forth, and stand upon the mount before the Lord. And, behold, the Lord passed by, and a great and strong wind rent the mountains, and brake in pieces the rocks before the Lord; but the Lord was not in the wind: and after the wind an earthquake; but the Lord was not in the earthquake: and after the earthquake a fire; but the Lord was not in the fire: and after the fire **a still small voice**" (1 Kgs 19:11–12).

33. Reading: 2 Kings 17

Answer: (a) Unfaithful **Israel** was "rent from the house of David" (17:21) and carried off into exile by the Assyrians. Its people were never heard from again. The "ten lost tribes of Israel" are Reuben, Simeon, Issachar, Zebulun, Dan, Naphtali, Gad, Asher, and the two Rachel tribes, Ephraim and Manasseh. All that was left was Judah, the small tribe of Benjamin (not even worthy of a mention by the writer of this chapter), and whatever Levites lived in Judah (the priestly tribe being scattered among all the tribes).

Israel and its capital Samaria were repopulated by the Assyrians with foreigners from other conquered lands, and the territory was henceforth known as Samaria. A priest was sent to instruct these new settlers "in how they should fear the Lord" (17:28), and they created their own hybrid version of worship which was controversial down through the time of Jesus.

The fate of the ten lost tribes has stirred countless theories. The Ethiopians claim descent; Ethiopian Orthodox churches by ancient tradition place an ark for the Torah beside the tabernacle for the Eucharist on their altars. Other claims are more far-fetched, ranging from the aboriginal North American tribes to the original occupiers of Japan. The Jewish historian Josephus believed that they survived beyond the Euphrates and had rebuilt themselves into a powerful nation. Another theory was that they became the Scythians, situated north of the Black Sea, and that these in turn became the Saxons, or "sons of Isaac," and these in turn became the modern English.

The truth is duller by being altogether natural: the Israelites were settled in modern Turkey and Syria, intermarried, and assimilated into the native populations. They "vanished" into history as countless other displaced tribes have disappeared before and since. Two centuries later the tribe of Judah would similarly be carried into exile by the Babylonians, but it would be careful not to assimilate. The *unnatural* determination of the Jews to keep faith with their God, their culture, and their tribe is why we read the Old Testament today.

We know for certain of only one descendent of the ten tribes: Anna, who served the Temple and prophesied that Jesus would bring redemption (Luke 2:26), is identified as being of the lost tribe of Asher.

34. Reading: 2 Kings 19
Answer: (d) As Isaiah prophesied, Judah was spared the fate of Israel. When the Assyrians besieged Jerusalem, "**the angel of the Lord went out, and smote** in the camp of the Assyrians an hundred fourscore and five thousand: and when they arose early in the morning, behold, they were all dead corpses" (19:35).

Historians have surmised that a plague struck the enemy army. However, when the Bible means "plague," it says "plague." In addition to the ten plagues of Egypt, plagues were used five times by God to punish various transgressions before this incident. In this case, divine intervention was direct —and effective.

Sennacherib was not successful in his sieges. Herodotus tells us that before his attack on Pelusium, which commanded the entrance into Egypt, "there came in the night, a multitude of field mice, which devoured all the quivers and bowstrings of the [Assyrians], and ate the thongs by which they managed their shields. Next morning they commenced their flight, and great multitudes fell, as they had no arms with which to defend themselves" (*Euterpe*, 141).

Whether this plague of mice occurred after the Assyrian king bypassed Jerusalem and the two incidents in later years were somehow confused, we do not know. The Assyrian records do not help: those so far unearthed from the reign of Sennacherib only speak of his victories. While they mention a besieged Jerusalem, they do not say why the siege was lifted.

35. Reading: 2 Kings 22

Answer: (a) "And Hilkiah the high priest said unto Shaphan the scribe, I have found **the book of the Law** in the house of the Lord" (22:8). The book, which was probably Deuteronomy, must have been hidden decades or even centuries before to preserve it from the vagaries of religious policy under the not-always-faithful kings. Its discovery in 621 B.C., more than three hundred years after the death of Solomon, caused a reformation: Idols were swept away, pagan practices were stomped out, and a great celebration was held on Passover: "Surely there was not holden such a passover from the days of the judges that judged Israel . . ." (23:22). But as the prophetess Huldah warned (22:17), even this was not enough to avoid the judgment that had already been leveled against Judah.

36. Reading: 2 Kings 24–25

Answer: (a) **Nebuchadnezzar** was not to be tampered with, as the prophet Jeremiah warned and two successive kings learned. Judah found itself caught between a weakened Egypt and an aggressive Babylon. Attempting to protect some vestige of independence, Judah's kings rebelled twice against Babylonian suzerainty. The second time was more than enough for the Babylonian king: Jerusalem was burnt to the ground, and its remaining people taken into exile.

37. Reading: Ezra 3–6
Answer: (b) The rebuilding of the Temple was a monumental undertaking in such a devastated and depopulated land as Judah. It was opposed at every turn by the **Samaritans,** who, if we were to hear their side of the story (which we don't), were greatly offended by the high-handed and snobbish Jews. The Samaritans were now the natives; after sixty years, the Jews were now the foreigners in their own country (anything familiar here?). The Samaritans seemed to try to make the best of a bad situation by offering to help: "Let us build with you: for we seek your God, as ye do, and we do sacrifice . . ." (4:2). But the Judan returnees had been coalescing in their captivity rather than assimilating, and they had reached a turning point. Their devotion to God would never again be compromised, and that meant they would never again allow the influence of alien thoughts or ideas of worship. As a result, conflicts, objections, and diplomatic wrangling delayed construction thirteen years. Finally the Temple was finished in the sixth year of Darius, and the people "kept the dedication of this house of God with joy" (6:16).

38. Reading: Nehemiah 8
Answer: (b) "And all the people gathered themselves together as one man into the street that was before the water gate; and they spake unto Ezra the scribe to bring **the book of the Law of Moses,** which the Lord had commanded to Israel" (8:1). Ezra proceeded to read from morning to midday for seven straight days; each day he and the Levites explained what he had read. The people gathered and listened and learned.

This was perhaps the beginning of Judaism as a religion. The ordinances of God were proclaimed, expounded upon, and explained as an instruction—or to use the Hebrew, as *Torah*.

Answers to CHAPTER **4**:

"THE WISDOM BOOKS"

≈≈≈

page 57

MEMORABLE COMMENTS

1. Reading: Job 14
Answer: (c) Job used this poignant phrase as a metaphor for death by utter exhaustion: "But man dieth, and wasteth away: yea, **man giveth up the ghost** . . ." (14:10). In Mark 15:37, the King James translators apply the same phrase with a slightly different touch: "And Jesus cried with a loud voice, and gave up the ghost." Not only are we to understand that Jesus was exhausted by his Passion, but that he was freely surrendering his life; to the translators he didn't just die, he *gave up* his life.

The Revised Standard has Job say, "humans expire." It also says Jesus "breathed his last." All other recent translations have followed its prosaic lead, with a loss not only in the richness of our language but in the meaning as well.

2. Reading: Job 19
Answer: (b) The saying has come down to us with a change of prepositions. Job actually said, "I am escaped *with* **the skin of my teeth**" (19:20).

3. Reading: Job 19
Answer: (a) "For **I know that my redeemer liveth,** and that he shall stand at the latter day upon the earth . . ." (Job 19:25). The verses 19–27 are a ringing affirmation of the

Messiah and his Resurrection: "And though after my skin worms destroy this body, yet in my flesh shall I see God" (19:26). Handel transformed this few verses into one of the great moments in his oratorio, *Messiah.*

4. Reading: Job 38
Answer: (a) **"Gird up now thy loins like a man;** for I will demand of thee, and answer thou me" (Job 38:2). In other words, get ready to stand up and be counted. To "gird up thy loins" means to pull up your long tunic and stuff it in your belt. The loose, flowing garments of biblical times would have been an encumbrance to anyone ready to take action or meet a challenge.

5. Reading: Psalm 8, Matthew 21
Answer: (b) **"Out of the mouth of babes** and sucklings has thou ordained strength because of thine enemies . . ." (8:2). The Hebrew original is confused, and the literal translation of King James reflects it. Jesus, who spoke Aramaic, quoted the Greek of the Septuagint translation when he said, "Yea; have ye never read, 'Out of the mouth of babes and sucklings thou has perfected praise'?" (Matt 21:16). Regardless of the confusion in the original, the phrase became one of the most famous oral sayings of all time.

6. Reading: Psalm 17
Answer: (a) When David wrote, "Keep me as **the apple of the eye,** hide me under the shadow of thy wings" (Ps 17:8), he was using a common metaphor of the time. The pupil of the eye, its most sensitive part and hence the one most in need of protection, was thought to be shaped like an apple. To treat someone as the "apple of the eye" was to treat them tenderly as having great value. The phrase is so apt it appears four other times in the Old Testament.

7. Reading: Luke 23, Psalm 31
Answer: (b) The Latin title of Psalm 31 is "In Te, Domine, Speravi"—"In thee, O Lord, have I hoped"—which expresses the spirit of faith with which Jesus confronted his death. It is from verse 5 of this same psalm that he quotes in

saying his very last words on the cross: "**Into thine hand I commit my spirit:** thou hast redeemed me, O Lord God of truth" (Ps 31:5, Luke 23:46).

8. Reading: Psalm 37
Answer: (a) "But **the meek shall inherit the earth,** and shall delight themselves in the abundance of peace" (Ps 37:11). Jesus quoted this psalm in the Beatitudes. (See Matt 5:5.)

9. Reading: Psalm 55
Answer: (c) The Psalmist, and in this case the author seems certain to be David, says of this unnamed adversary that he was "a man mine equal, my guide, and mine acquaintance. We took sweet counsel together and walked unto the house of God in company" (Ps 55:13–14). But the friend turned out to be a traitor. "**The words of his mouth were smoother than butter,** but war was in his heart: his words were softer than oil, yet were they drawn swords" (Ps 55:21). One can only speculate as to the man's identity, but from the evidence of the psalm ("mine equal") I would guess a subject king who rebelled.

10. Reading: Proverbs 8, 9
Answer: (a) This ode to Lady Wisdom lays layer of metaphor upon metaphor, and none is more famous than the metaphor of the house built on "**the seven pillars**" of wisdom (Prov 9:2). Rabbinic commentary has identified the pillars with the seven patriarchs: Adam, Noah, Abraham, Isaac, Jacob, Joseph, and Judah. St. Augustine thought they prefigured the seven churches of Revelation, thereby symbolizing the universal Church. T. E. Lawrence ("of Arabia") entitled his autobiography *The Seven Pillars of Wisdom*.

11. Reading: Ecclesiastes 1
Answer: (c) "**and there is no new thing under the sun**" (Eccl 1:9). As one commentator noted, even that statement probably wasn't new.

12. Reading: Ecclesiastes 9
Answer: (b) "I returned, and saw under the sun, that **the race is not to the swift,** nor the battle to the strong, neither

yet bread to the wise, nor yet riches to men of understanding, nor yet favour to men of skill; but time and chance happeneth to them all" (Eccl 9:11).

THE PSALMIST'S FAMOUS PHRASES

13. (b) (Psalm 2:1) "Why do the heathen rage, and imagine **a vain thing.**" This phrase was made famous by Handel in his *Messiah.* The human king portrayed in Psalm 2 prefigures the divine king; the Davidic line becomes the Messianic line. (See Heb 1:5.)

14. (c) (Psalm 8:5) "For thou has made him a little lower than **the angels . . .**" (After his European tour, Mark Twain commented, "A little lower than the angels, and a little higher than the French.")

15. (b) (Psalm 18:10) "He rode upon a cherub and did fly: yea, he did fly upon **the wings of the wind.**" The contemporary image of cherubs as rosy-cheeked, fat little cupids (as in *cherubic* smile) is a far cry from the biblical image of them as strong, winged warriors (see Gen 3:24, when they make their first appearance). In this psalm they are directly connected with the power of the storm and with terrific natural phenomena—earthquakes, thunder, hail, fire.

16. (d) (Psalm 19:1) "The heavens declare the glory of God; and the firmament showeth **his handiwork.**"

17. (b) (Psalm 24:1) "The earth is the Lord's, and the fullness thereof; the world, and **they that dwell within.**"

18. (b) (Psalm 33:3) "Sing unto him **a new song.**"

19. (c) (Psalm 46:10) "Be still, and know **that I am God.**"

20. (d) (Psalm 90:9) "We spend our years as **a tale that is told.**" Shakespeare builds on the thought in *Macbeth,* adding

an author: "Life . . . is a tale told by an idiot, full of sound and fury, signifying nothing."

21. (a) (Psalm 90:10) "The days of our years are **three-score and ten.**"

22. (d) (Psalm 111:10) "So teach us to **number our days,** that we may apply our hearts to wisdom." And so it is that we know our days are numbered.

23. (a) (Psalm 116:11) "I said in my haste, **all men are liars.**" The Psalmist does not say why he reached the hasty conclusion, although we can guess.

24. (d) (Psalm 116:15) "Precious in the sight of the Lord is **the death of his saints.**"

25. (a) (Psalm 118: 22) "The stone which the builders refused is become the **head stone of the corner.**" Jesus interpreted this passage to prophesy his rejection by the leaders of the Jews (Matt 21:42). In his first Epistle, St. Peter quotes Isaiah's allusion to the same verse: "Behold, I lay in Zion for a foundation a stone, a tried stone, a precious corner stone, a sure foundation: he that believeth shall not make haste [be forced to flee]" (Isa 28:16).

26. (c) (Psalm 118:26) "Blessed is he who comes **in the name of the Lord.**" See Matthew 21:9.

27. (a) (Psalm 119:105) "Thy word is a lamp unto my feet, and a **light unto my path.**"

28. (d) (Psalm 121:1) "I will lift up mine eyes unto the hills, from whence cometh my **help.**"

29. (a) (Psalm 122:1) "I was glad when they said unto me, Let us go **into the house of the Lord.**"

30. (b) (Psalm 126:5) "They that sow in tears shall reap in **joy.**" This may have been the song sung by those returning from the Babylonian Captivity.

31. (a) (Psalm 127:1) "Except that the Lord build the house, they labor in vain that build it; except the Lord keep the city **the watchman waketh but in vain.**" John F. Kennedy intended to use this text in the luncheon speech he was to give on the day he was assassinated.

32. (d) (Psalm 137:1) "By the rivers of Babylon, there we sat down, yea, we wept, when we remembered **Zion.**" Equally poignant are verses 4 ("How shall we sing the Lord's song in a strange land?") and 5 ("It I forget thee, O Jerusalem, let my right hand forget its cunning").

33. (c) (Psalm 139: 14) "I will praise thee; for I am **fearfully and wonderfully made . . .**"

34. (d) (Psalm 146:3) "Put not your trust in **princes,** nor in the son of man, in whom there is no help."

35. (d) (Psalm 150:6) "Let every thing that hath breath **praise the Lord.**" A fitting end for the book of Psalms.

THE PSALM OF THE CROSS

36. (c) **The darkness over the land.** Psalm 22 contains seven prophetic descriptions of Jesus on the cross.
The First: Verse 7. "All they that see me laugh me to score: they shoot out the lip, they shake the head . . ."
"And they that passed by him reviled him, wagging their heads . . ." (Matt 27:39).
The Second: Verse 8. ". . . saying, He trusted on the Lord that he would deliver him: let him deliver him, seeing he delighted in him."
"He trusted in God; let him deliver him now, if he will have him: for he said, I am the Son of God" (Matt 27: 43).
The Third: Verse 15. "My strength is dried up like a

potsherd; and my tongue cleaveth to my jaws; and thou hast brought me into the dust of death."

"After this, Jesus knowing that all things were now accomplished, that the Scripture might be fulfilled, said, I thirst" (John 19:28–29).

The Fourth: Verse 16. ". . . they pierced my hands and my feet."

"And when they were come to the place which is called Calvary, there they crucified him . . ." (Luke 23: 33).

The Fifth: Verse 17. "I may tell [count] all my bones."

"Then came the soldiers, and brake the legs of the first, and of the other which was crucified with him. But when they came to Jesus, and saw he was dead already, they brake not his legs" (John 19: 23–24). See also Psalm 34:20: "He keepeth all his bones: not one of them is broken."

The Sixth: Verse 17. ". . . they look and stare upon me."

"And sitting down they watched him there" (Matt 27:36).

The Seventh: Verse 18. "They part my garments among them, and cast lots upon my vesture."

"Then the soldiers, when they had crucified Jesus, took his garments, and made four parts, to every soldier a part; and also his coat: now the coat was without seam, woven from the top throughout. They said therefore among themselves, Let us not rend it, but cast lots for it, whose it shall be. . . . These things therefore the soldiers did" (John 19:23–24).

THE TWENTY-THIRD PSALM

37. The Lord is my *shepherd;* I shall not *want.*

He maketh me to lie down *in green pastures:* he leadeth me beside the *still waters.* He *restoreth* my soul: he leadeth me in the *paths* of righteousness for *his name's* sake. Yea, though I walk through the *valley of the shadow of death,* I will fear *no evil:* for thou art with me; thy *rod and thy staff* they comfort me. Thou preparest a *table* before me in the presence of *mine enemies:* thou anointest my head with *oil;* my *cup* runneth over.

Surely *goodness* and *mercy* shall follow me all the days of my life: and I will dwell *in the house of the Lord* for ever.

PROVERBIAL STATEMENTS

38. (c) (Proverbs 4:7) "Wisdom is the principal thing: therefore get wisdom, and with all thy getting get **understanding.**"

39. (b) (Proverbs 5:3) "The lips of a strange woman drop as a honeycomb, and her mouth is **smoother than oil.**"

40. (a) (Proverbs 6:6) "Go to the ant, thou sluggard, consider her ways, and **be wise.**"

41. (c) (Proverbs 6:27–28) "Can a man take fire to his bosom, and his **clothes not be burned?**"

42. (d) (Proverbs 7:21–22) "With her fair speech she caused him to yield, with the flattering of her lips she forced him. He goeth after her straightaway, **as an ox goeth to the slaughter.**"

43. (a) (Proverbs 9:17) "Stolen waters are sweet, and bread eaten in secret is **pleasant.**"

44. (d) (Proverbs 11:4) "In the multitude of counsellors there is **safety.**"

45. (b) (Proverbs 11:22) "As a jewel of gold in a swine's snout, so is a fair woman which is **without discretion.**"

46. (c) (Proverbs 11:29) "He that troubleth his own house shall **inherit the wind.**"

47. (b) (Proverbs 13:12) "Hope deferred maketh **the heart sick.**"

48. (a) (Proverbs 13:19) "Desire accomplished is **sweet to the soul.**"

49. (d) (Proverbs 13:24) "He that spareth the rod **hateth his son.**" This has been boiled down in English to "spare the rod and spoil the child." But the original is much more emphatic: The parent who does not discipline his children does not love them.

50. (c) (Proverbs 15:1) "A soft answer turneth away **wrath.**"

51. (b) (Proverbs 16:18) "Pride goeth before **destruction,** and a haughty spirit before a fall."

52. (c) (Proverbs 19:4) "Wealth maketh many **friends.**" Proverbs is nothing if not realistic.

53. (b) (Proverbs 22:6) "Train up a child in the way he should go; and when he is old, *he* will **not depart from it.**"

54. (d) (Proverbs 22:29) "Seeth thou a man diligent in his business? He shall **stand before kings.**"

55. (b) (Proverbs 23:2) "Put a knife to thy throat, if thou be a man given to **appetite.**"

56. (a) (Proverbs 25:21) "If thine enemy be hungry **give him bread to eat;** and if he be thirsty, give him water to drink." The advice is for psychological, not charitable reasons: "For [then] thou shall heap coals of fire upon his head."

57. (d) (Proverbs 26:5) "Answer a fool according to his **folly.**"

58. (b) (Proverbs 27:5) "Open rebuke is better than **secret love.**"

59. (b) (Proverbs 29:18) "Where there is no vision, **the people perish.**"

60. (a) (Proverbs 30:20) "Such is the way of an adulterous woman; she eateth, and wipeth her mouth, and saith, I **have done no wickedness.**" The wonderful thing about the King James Version is that its images work sometimes when the phrasing, taken literally, makes no sense. On a literal level, eating, wiping, and saying have no relationship with one another, but taken together, they conjure up a vision of the woman as real as if she were sitting across the table.

61. (b) (Proverbs 31:10) "Who can find a virtuous woman? for her price is far above **rubies.**"

SING ALONG WITH THE SONG OF SONGS

62. (c) (Songs 1:2) "Let him kiss me with the kisses of his mouth: for thy love is better than **wine.**"

63. (b) (Songs 2:1) "I am the rose of Sharon, and **the lily of the valley.**"

64. (d) (Songs 8:6) "Set me as a seal upon thy **heart.**"

65. (a) (Songs 8:7) "Many waters cannot quench **love.**"

FAMOUS PEOPLE

66: Reading: Job
Answer: (b) In fact, no one—including God—paid the slightest attention to **Elihu,** who was neither introduced in the beginning nor answered at the end. This has led to speculation that his speech was an interpolation by a pious editor who was so offended by Job's problem he felt a need to answer it, a need apparently not felt by the Lord himself.

67. Reading: Job 42
Answer: (d) The Lord spoke to Eliphaz, "My wrath is kindled against thee, and thy two friends: for ye have not spoken of me the thing that is right, as my servant Job hath . . .

offer up for yourselves a burnt offering; and my servant Job shall pray for you . . ." (Job 42:7–8).

68. Reading: Psalm 34, 1 Samuel 21

Answer: (b) "Abilemech" seems to be an honorific accorded the king of the Philistines, just as Pharaoh was for the Egyptians or Caesar for the Romans. Both Abraham and Isaac had dealings with an Abilemech in their own times. In this case, the given name of Abilemech (not to be confused with Ahimelech the priest) was Achish, to whom David fled to escape Saul's murderous jealousy. When Achish discovered David's true identity, David **feigned madness** to escape. It was a terrifying moment for David, surrounded as he was by harm on all sides, and Psalm 34 is his testimony to God's saving him, containing that wonderful phrase, "O taste and see that the Lord is good."

69. Reading: Psalm 110, Genesis 14, Hebrews 5:1–10

Answer: (c) "The Lord hath sworn and will not repent: Thou art a priest for ever after the order of **Melchizedek**" (Ps 110:4).

Answers to CHAPTER 5:

"THE PROPHETS"

≈≈≈

page 79

MEMORABLE COMMENTS

1. Reading: Isaiah 1
Answer: (b) **"Come now, and let us reason together, saith the Lord . . ."** (Isa 1:18). This was Lyndon Johnson's favorite phrase, which he often quoted just before he was about to twist some congressional arms.

2. Reading: Isaiah 40
Answer: (a) A change in prepositions but no change in meaning has occurred since Isaiah wrote "Behold the nations are as **a drop of a bucket,** and are counted as the small dust . . ." (Isa 40:15).

3. Reading: Isaiah 52
Answer: (c) To **"see eye to eye"** (Isa 52:8) therefore has come to mean to be of one mind.

4. Reading: Isaiah 53
Answer: (b) ". . . he is brought **as a lamb to the slaughter."** (Isa 53:7). Chapter 53 deserves to be read and re-read for its depiction of the sufferings of Christ.

5. Reading: Isaiah 65
Answer: (b) Isaiah felt about **holier-than-thou** types

the same as most of us do, but he was the first to apply the label.

6. Reading: Jeremiah 13
Answer: (c) Not many of us believe **a leopard can change his spots,** and neither did Jeremiah.

7. Reading: Ezekiel 18
Answer: (c) In a vision, the Lord said to Ezekiel that the people say, "The fathers have eaten **sour grapes,** and the children's teeth are set on edge." He warned that this old proverb should never be repeated, "For all souls are mine: as the soul of the father so like the soul of the son is mine; the soul that sinneth, it shall die" (Ezek 18:2–4). In other words, the present punishments of Israel cannot be blamed on the sins of past generations. Every person must assume responsibility for his own actions.

At roughly the same time that Ezekiel was pronouncing this judgment in the sixth century B.C., Aesop was writing his fables, one of which concerned a fox who, failing to reach some grapes that were too high for him, said that they were probably sour grapes anyway. So when a person disparages something he can't have anyway, we call it *sour grapes.* Given the importance of the grape in ancient cultures, the use of the phrase must have had a variety of meanings, all of them roughly connoting the same thing: not good.

8. Reading: Daniel 2
Answer: (d) Daniel saw an image whose "head was of gold, his breast and his arms of silver, his belly and his thighs of brass, his legs of iron, his feet part of iron and part of **clay**" (Dan 2:32–33). After Nebuchadnezzar's Babylon would come an inferior kingdom of silver (Persia), a third of brass (the Greece of Alexander the Great), and a fourth of iron (Rome). "But in the days of these kings [those of iron] shall the God of heaven set up a kingdom, which shall never be destroyed . . ." (2:44). A stone cut from the mountain (Christ) would fall and break apart the great image (2:45). So when the mighty fall, we remind ourselves that everyone has feet of clay.

9. Reading: Daniel 5

Answer: (b) Belshazzar, who showed no respect for the God of the Hebrews, profaned the silver and golden cups taken from the Temple at Jerusalem by ordering his companions to drink wine from them while toasting Babylonian idols. He and his court were then amazed to see a disembodied wrist **writing on the wall,** "MENE, MENE, TEKEL, UPHARSIN," which the prophet Daniel interpreted to mean, "You have been weighed in the balance and found wanting" (Dan 5:25–28). That night Belshazzar was slain, and Babylon fell to the Persians.

10. Reading: Daniel 7

Answer: (c) This vision is subject to various interpretations, with the most common equating the four beasts with the four empires suggested by the great image. It is, however, the first time this title of **"Ancient of days"** is applied to God.

11. Reading: Joel 3

Answer: (a) This is an argument for the later dating of Joel, for it seems a deliberate play on the famous Isaiaic prediction that ". . . they shall beat their swords into plowshares, and their spears into pruninghooks: nation shall not make war against nation, neither shall they learn war any more" (Isa 2:4). (Isaiah is repeated verbatim in Micah 4:3, by the way, which means it is an interpolation in one or the other.) Joel twisted it around when he warned the Gentiles to **"beat your plowshares into swords,** and your pruninghooks into spears: let the weak say, I am strong" (Joel 3:10).

FAMOUS AND NOT-SO-FAMOUS PEOPLE

12. Reading: Isaiah 14

Answer: (a) In this contemptuous passage, Isaiah (or a later writer who inserted this chapter into Isaiah) revels in the fall of the Babylonian king, sarcastically calling him **"Lucifer"** or "Shining One" (Isa 14:12), which may have actually been a Babylonian epithet, in the same way Louis XIV was called the "Sun King." Like the morning star that falls from heaven, the

Babylonian king has fallen from absolute power to the depths of hell.

In Luke 10:18, when the disciples sent out as missionaries return rejoicing that they are able to banish evil spirits, Jesus seems unimpressed, commenting, "I beheld Satan as lightning fall from heaven." This comment about Satan's fall ("as lightning") led to identification with Isaiah 14, and the name "Lucifer" was added to the titles of the Evil One.

13. Reading: Isaiah 36–37

Answer: (c) "Behold, I will send a blast upon him, and he shall hear **a rumour,** and return to his own land . . ." (Isa 37:7). Sure enough, the army commander withdrew to find Sennacherib fighting against Libnah with a rumor of an imminent attack by the king of "Ethiopia" (Egypt).

14. Reading: Hebrews 11

Answer: (b) In Hebrews 11:37, the fates of the prophets are listed: "They were stoned, they were **sawn asunder,** were tempted, were slain by the sword . . ." The phrase "sawn asunder" refers to the Jewish legend that Isaiah was murdered by King Manesseh, who indeed persecuted the prophets. As the story goes, Isaiah fled the king's troops sent to arrest him and hid in a tree, which the soldiers then sawed in half. As far as biblical testimony goes, there is no mention of Isaiah after the failure of Sennacherib's siege of Jerusalem. He could have lived into the reign of Manesseh.

15. Reading: Jeremiah 27

Answer: (c) Jeremiah **made and wore a yoke** (Jer 27:2) to symbolize that the nations were to be under the yoke of Babylon and rebellion would be not only futile but foolhardy. Naturally, this was regarded as unpatriotic.

16. Reading: Jeremiah 28

Answer: (b) Hanniah told the people what they wanted to hear, that the yoke of Babylon would be broken, and to symbolize this he took hold of and broke Jeremiah's yoke. For his falsely raising the hopes of the people, Jeremiah pronounced his **death,** and sure enough Hanniah died the same year (Jer 28: 16–17).

17. Reading: Jeremiah 31

Answer: (b) **Rachel** was the mother of Benjamin and Joseph, patriarch of the two tribes of Ephriam and Manesseh, the two major tribes of Israel, both of which were carried off to exile in the Assyrian captivity. "A voice was heard in Ramah, lamentation, and bitter weeping, Rachel weeping for her children refused to be comforted . . ." (Jer 31:15). But the Lord promised that one day Israel would be restored.

Matthew saw this passage as a prophecy of the slaughter of the innocents under Herod (Matt 2:17).

18. Reading: Jeremiah 36

Answer: (c) The high regard in which **Baruch** was held is indicated by the number of writings attributed to him, collected in the apocryphal Book of Baruch.

19. Reading: Hosea 1–3

Answer: (c) "Go, take unto thee **a wife of whoredoms** and children of whoredoms: for the land hath committed great whoredom, departing from the Lord" (Hos 1:2). Hosea's patient suffering of his wife's infidelities was to be a symbol of God's patience for unfaithful Israel.

20. Reading: Jonah

Answer: (a) Everyone in the book of Jonah—the rough sailors, the fish, the Gentiles in Ninevah—does God's will, except for the hero of the tale, **Jonah,** who tries to escape his calling.

PROPHETIC STATEMENTS: TRUE OR FALSE

21. In the last days:

a. **True.** ". . . and he shall build the temple of the Lord" (Zech 6:12).

b. **False.** "And it shall be said in that day, Lo, this is our God; we have waited for him and he will save us . . ." (Isa 25:9).

c. **True.** "The wolf shall also dwell with the lamb . . ." (Isa 11:6).

d. **False.** "For then will I turn to the people a pure language, that they may all call upon the name of the Lord, to serve him with one consent" (Zeph 3:9).

e. **True.** "But they shall sit every man under his vine and under his fig tree; and none shall make them afraid: for the mouth of the Lord of hosts hath spoken it." (Mic 4:4).

f. **False.** ". . . for out of Zion shall go forth the law, and the word of the Lord from Jerusalem" (Isa 2:3).

g. **True.** ". . . for the child shall die a hundred years old" (Isa 65:20).

h. **False.** "And the work of righteousness shall be peace; and the effect of righteousness quietness and assurance for ever" (Isa 32:17).

i. **True.** "I will bring thy seed from the east, and gather thee from the west; I will say to the north, Give up; and to the south, Keep not back: bring my sons from far, and my daughters from the ends of the earth" (Isa 43:5–6).

j. **True.** "Afterward shall the children of Israel return, and seek the Lord their God, and David their king, and shall fear the Lord and his goodness in the later days" (Hos 3:5).

22. The Messiah will:

a. **True.** "Behold I will send my messenger, and he shall prepare the way before me . . ." (Mal 3:1).

b. **True.** "But thou, Bethlehem Ephratah, though thou be little among the thousands of Judah, yet out of thee shall he come forth unto me that is to be rule in Israel; whose goings forth have been from of old, from everlasting" (Mic 5:2).

c. **False.** "The people that walked in darkness have seen a great light: they that dwell in the land of the shadow of death, upon them hath the light shined" (Isa 9:2).

d. **True.** "He is despised and rejected of men . . ." (Isa 53:3).

e. **True.** ". . . behold, thy King cometh unto thee: he is just, and having salvation; lowly and riding upon an ass, and upon a colt the foal of an ass" (Zech 9:9).

f. **False.** ". . . smite the shepherd, and the sheep shall be scattered . . ." (Zech 13:7).

g. **False.** "And he made his grave with the wicked and with the rich in his death . . ." (Isa 53:9).

h. **True.** "And he bare the sin of many, and made intercession for the transgressors" (Isa 53:12).

i. **True.** "And so they weighted for my price thirty pieces of silver" (Zech 11:12).

j. **True.** "And the Gentiles shall come to thy light, and kings to the brightness of thy rising" (Isa 60:3).

k. **False.** "He was oppressed and afflicted, yet he opened not his mouth . . ." (Isa 53:7).

l. **False.** " his visage was so marred more than any man . . ." (Isa 52:14).

Answers to CHAPTER 6:

"THE GOSPELS"

≈≈≈

page 95

MEMORABLE COMMENTS

1. Reading: Matthew 5–7

Answer: (c) In telling his disciples, "Beware of false prophets, **which come to you in sheep's clothing, but inwardly they are ravening wolves**" (Matt 7:15), Jesus was relying on one of the oldest metaphors of the ancient world. A fable called "The Wolf in Sheep's Clothing" was attributed to Aesop ca. 550 B.C., although it may be much older. Ancients believed, and it may be true, that wolves would strip the skin off a dead sheep and use it as covering to sneak into a flock.

2. Reading: Matthew 5–7

Answer: (c) Because of its use in the preservation of meat, salt was one of the most valuable commodities in the ancient world. But when the salt lost its "savour" (strength), it was worthless. So, Jesus told his disciples, would it be with them: they were the instruments for the salvation of the world, but if they lost their faith, they were nothing. To call a person "**the salt of the earth**" remains one of the highest compliments that can be paid.

3. Reading: Mark 3

Answer: (b) The press of the first crowd to gather around him and its response to his words affected Jesus deeply, and he may have seemed to go into a mystical state. "And when his friends heard of it, they went out and lay hold of him; for they said, He is **beside himself**" (Mark 3:21).

4. Reading: Luke 4

Answer: (d) One can only imagine the reaction in his hometown synagogue when Jesus quoted the prophecy of Isaiah and then pronounced, "This day is this scripture fulfilled in your ears." Surprise at the "gracious words which proceeded out of his mouth" was mingled with skepticism as neighbor turned to neighbor and asked, "Is not this Joseph's son?" Noting their puzzlement, Jesus quoted the old maxim "**Physician, heal thyself**" (Luke 4:23) as he guessed that they were wondering why he had performed no miracles in his own hometown, if it were really true that he had performed them in Capernaum. He then went on to remark that "no prophet is accepted in his own country." Interestingly, all four Evangelists agree that Jesus said that a prophet is not honored or accepted in his own country, but only one quotes the maxim about healing oneself: it is, of course, Luke—the physician.

5. Reading: Mark 3

Answer: (b) Ridiculing the assertion by scribes from Jerusalem that only Satan could have empowered him to drive out demons, Jesus asked, "How can Satan drive out Satan? **If a house be divided against itself, that house cannot stand.** And if Satan rise up against himself, and be divided, he cannot stand" (Mark 3:25–26). Abraham Lincoln made memorable use of the phrase in making the same point about a nation divided into half-slave and half-free.

6. Reading: Matthew 12
Answer: (c) In Matthew's version of the same incident, Jesus scolded the same scribes—here referred to as Pharisees—for blasphemy against the Holy Spirit, the one unforgivable sin. They should have recognized him for who he was "**. . . for the tree is known by its fruits**" (Matt 12:33).

7. Reading: Matthew 16
Answer: (b) When the Pharisees tested Jesus by asking him to give a sign from heaven, Jesus derided them, saying "When it is evening, ye say, '**It will be fair weather, for the sky is red**' " (Matt 16:2). The whole exchange is rendered more colloquially in the New American Bible: "In the evening you say, 'Red sky at night, the day will be bright'; but in the morning, 'Sky red and gloomy, the day will be stormy.' If you know how to interpret the look of the sky, can you not read the signs of the times?" No wonder Jesus was able to attract his disciples: he obviously knew the language of fishermen.

8. Reading: Matthew 22
Answer: (d) In this parable, Jesus warned his listeners to prepare for the last judgment, where they would find "**many are called, but few are chosen**" (Matt 22:14). Note that the original notables invited to the banquet for the king's son didn't show up, and their places were taken by common people pulled in off the streets. The Messiah of Israel might have expected to be embraced by priests and rulers and the learned of his generation; his followers, however, were of the most common class, even including the despised. Even if you never expected to be among those to welcome the Messiah, Jesus was saying to his followers, you should rise to the role that has been thrust upon you.

9. Reading: Luke 12
Answer: (c) The rich man decided to enjoy his good luck and to "**eat, drink, and be merry**" (Luke 12:20). He had

laid up his treasure for himself, and not for God. And God answered him by saying, "Thou fool, this night thy soul shall be required of thee."

The philosophy of "eat, drink, and be merry" has its ups and downs in the Bible. Ecclesiastes (8:15) in his world-weary way positively endorsed it, "because a man hath no better thing under the sun." Isaiah (22:13) denounced it as blasphemous, with the addition of the well-known appendage "for tomorrow we shall die."

10. Reading: John 12

Answer: (d) Mary had poured an expensive ointment on her Lord's feet, and Judas upbraided her for not selling it and using the money instead for the needy. Jesus said, "Let her alone: against the day of my burying hath she kept this. **For the poor always ye have with you;** but me ye have not always" (John 12:7–8). Given his extensive knowledge of Scripture, Jesus may have been referring to Deuteronomy 15:11: "The poor shall never cease out of the land."

In an aside, John notes that Judas cared nothing for the poor, but wanted to sell the oil to replenish funds he had stolen from the common purse.

FAMOUS PEOPLE

11. Reading: Matthew 1

Answer: (a) Four women are mentioned in Matthew's genealogy of Jesus: Tamar, Rahab, Ruth, and "her that had been the wife of Urias," i.e., Bath-sheeba. This is a very interesting selection from the genealogical line, including as it does a woman who played a prostitute, a woman who was a prostitute, a foreigner, and an adulteress. Were these selected because of their biblical fame? Surely **Sarah** and Rebekah and Rachel were more famous and, indeed, more important. Was Matthew subtly making a larger point about the descent of the Savior? The selected women shared only one trait: by their actions, they redeemed themselves. Tamar played the prostitute to bear children to Judah and continue the line, and even Judah said "she hath been more righteous than I." Rahab the prostitute of Jericho sheltered the spies of the invading Hebrews and was rewarded by Joshua. Ruth the Moabess chose to follow her Hebrew mother-in-law, Naomi. Bathsheeba, whom Matthew couldn't bring himself to mention by name, was helped by none other than the prophet Nathan (who had denounced her liaison with David) in making her son Solomon king of Israel. Keep in mind that Matthew himself had been a tax collector for the Romans, one of the most despised occupations of the period.

12. Reading: Matthew 1, Luke 1, Romans 5:18–19
Answer: (b) Both Joseph (Matt 1:21) and Mary (Luke 1:31) were told to name the child Jesus **"for he shall save his people from their sins."**

13. Reading: Luke 1
Answer: (a) When Zacharias had the temerity to question the announcement of the angel Gabriel that he would soon have a son he was **struck dumb.** Zacharias' question seemed perfectly reasonable: "Whereby shall I know this? for I am an old man, and my wife well stricken in years" (Luke 1:18). Six months later, after an even more remarkable announcement, the virgin Mary would ask a similar question: "How shall this be, seeing that I know not man" (Luke 1:34) and receive a gentle answer instead of a rebuke. Either the angel Gabriel had learned something about human denseness or he expected less from the young girl than from the aged priest.

14. Reading: Matthew 1
Answer: (b) "Then Joseph her husband, being a just man, and not willing to make her a publick example, was minded to put her away privily" (Matt 1:19). The betrothal in Palestine at this time was actually the first step in a two-step marriage, and under Mosaic law, Joseph had every right to call for a divorce. But "being a just man," he seems to have decided to quietly **call off the marriage.** Many reasons can be offered for his decision: He wanted to preserve his own reputation by not letting it get around that he had been cuckolded; he felt a moral and even legal obligation to divorce a woman who was bearing another man's child; he had no interest in a love-

less marriage and wanted to free Mary to marry the father of the child; he was utterly bewildered by Mary's explanation of her pregnancy but didn't want to expose her to public ridicule. Joseph's later actions, in inviting Mary to accompany him to the child's presentation in the Temple (an unnecessary and even unusual action for the time) and in upending his life to protect the child by fleeing to Egypt, show he deserved the compliment Matthew paid to him.

15. Reading: John 1, Exodus 12, Isaiah 53
Answer: (a) "Behold **the Lamb of God,** which taketh away the sin of the world" (John 1:29). John's sacrificial metaphor recalls the lamb "without blemish" whose blood protected the Israelites on the night of the first Passover (Exod 12:5, see also 1 Pet 1:19), as well as Isaiah's image of the suffering servant who "is brought as a lamb to the slaughter . . ." (Isa 53:7).

16. Reading: Matthew 4, Mark 1, Luke 5, John 1
Answer: (c) **Andrew** is featured in John as a follower of John the Baptist who becomes the first disciple of Jesus and informs his brother Simon that he has found the Messiah. His name occurs only twelve times in the Gospels, four of which are in lists of the apostles. Constantinople claimed him as its patron, perhaps in a bid for supremacy against Rome's Peter. He also became the patron saint of Scotland when a relic of his was taken there in the fourth century.

17. Reading: Mark 5
Answer: (a) Jesus raised three people from the dead: **the daughter of Jairus** (Mark 5:22), a widow's son (Luke 7:11), and Lazarus (John 11:38). In the first case, with Jairus' daughter, Jesus claimed she was only asleep, which led the family to scoff. It may have been that, so early in his ministry, Jesus was trying to downplay his powers.

18. Reading: Matthew 16, John 1
Answer: (b) In the most famous—and most important —pun in world history, Jesus rewards Simon's declaration of faith in him as the Son of the living God with ". . . thou art

Peter [the rock], and upon this rock I will build my church; and the gates of hell shall not prevail against it" (Matt 16:18). The King James translator of John's gospel retains the Greek word for rock, having Jesus say ". . . thou shalt be called Cephas" (John 1:42).

19. Reading: Mark 3
Answer: (c) The appellation of "**sons of thunder**" or "sons of trembling" may refer to their impetuosity. Luke relates that when certain Samaritan villages were unreceptive to the gospel, the brothers urged Jesus to bring down fire from heaven to consume them (Luke 9:54). There's also a certain brashness in their request to be seated to Jesus' right and left, respectively, when he reigns in his kingdom (Mark 10:35–37).

20. Reading: Mark 2
Answer: (b) Exodus 25:30 required that showbread be kept before the Tabernacle at all times and could be eaten only by the priests. In pointing out that the Law could be broken for the good of men, Jesus cited the story of **David,** who himself broke the Law in fleeing from Saul: ". . . he went into the house of God in the days of Abiathar the high priest, and did eat **the shewbread,** which is not lawful to eat . . ." (Mark 2: 26). Mark, in recounting Jesus' reply, got one detail wrong, though: it was Ahimelech, Abiathar's father, who was high priest at the time (see 1 Sam 21:6). Matthew and Luke recounted the same story but left out the name of the high priest, thereby avoiding the error.

21. Reading: Luke 8, Mark 16, Matthew 27, 28
Answer: (a) Luke identified among the followers of Jesus ". . . certain women, which had been **healed of evil spirits** and evil infirmities, Mary called Magdalene, out of whom went seven devils" (Luke 8:2). She was at the cross (Matt 27:56; Mark 15:40; John 19:25) and witnessed the burial of Jesus (Mark 15:42–47). She was either the first or among the first to learn of the Resurrection (Matt 27:61; Mark 16:1–8; Luke 24:3; John 20:1–2).
Nowhere in any of the Gospels is it even hinted at that Mary Magdalene could have been a prostitute, but the

identification of her with prostitution has endured throughout history, so much so that the word "magdalen" means a reformed prostitute. The error may have been begun by early attackers of Christianity, who accused Mary the mother of Jesus of adultery and often merged the two women into one. Or it may have begun because the Hebrew *m'gadd'la*, or hairdresser, was often a euphemism for prostitute. The confusion wasn't helped by early Church fathers who identified her with the account of the sinful woman that comes just before her name is mentioned in Luke's gospel (7:36–39). As a result, in artistic representations Mary Magdalene is pictured as a reformed sinner with weepy red eyes and a sorrowful expression, from which comes our word *maudlin*.

Isaac Asimov makes an interesting point about Mary Magdalene in connection with the skepticism shown by the disciples in Mark when she went to tell them of the Resurrection. Anyone infected with seven devils must have seemed under the burden of some severe form of mental illness. Although she had been cured by Jesus, it was likely she was not regarded as altogether reliable to those who had known her before. According to Mark, it was only after Jesus appeared to the eleven "as they sat at meat" (16:14) that the disciples believed.

22. Reading: Matthew 12, Luke 11
Answer: (d) "For as **Jonah** was three days and three nights in the whale's belly; so shall the Son of man be three days and three nights in the heart of the earth" (Matt 12:40, cf. Luke 11:30).

23. Reading: Matthew 14
Answer: (b) "And [Herod] said unto his servants, This is **John the Baptist;** he is risen from the dead; and therefore mighty works do show forth themselves in him" (Matt 14:2).

24. Reading: Mark 5
Answer: (c) "And he asked him, What is thy name? And he answered, saying, My name is **Legion:** for we are many" (Mark 5:9).

25. Reading: Luke 17:11–19

Answer: (a) This incident, where only the heretical foreigner—which was what Jews considered **Samaritans**—returned to give thanks to Jesus for healing him is a parable in itself, for it forecasts or perhaps is a commentary on the rejection of Jesus among the Jews and his acceptance only among the outcasts and Gentiles.

26. Reading: Luke 19: 1–10

Answer: (b) Jesus made the point about outcasts even more strongly by dining with Zacchaeus, the chief among the publicans—or **tax collectors**—of Jericho. To understand why tax collectors were so hated, one must understand the Roman system. To avoid bureaucracy, the Romans would simply give the tax franchise to a local citizen who would put up a surety or bond for a minimum amount to be collected; the difference between the amount actually collected and the minimum was then split, making it in the tax collector's best interest to squeeze every dime out of his territory. Indeed, Luke made a point of noting that Zacchaeus was rich. The described scene is wonderful: The short, rich tax collector can't see over the heads of his neighbors, so he clambers up a sycamore tree to get a view of the miracle worker, where Jesus spots him and invites himself to dinner. Hearing the murmuring against Jesus for deigning to enter such a house, Zacchaeus delivers an after-dinner speech defending his conduct, and apparently makes an impression, for he causes Jesus to make another of his famous puns, "This day is salvation come to this house . . ." (Luke 19:9). Salvation, of course, is the name *Jesus*.

27. Reading: John 7

Answer: (b) After its own soldiers refused to arrest Jesus (excusing themselves by saying, "Never man spake like this man"), the Sanhedrin was thrown into confusion, which **Nicodemus** bravely exploited by raising a point of law: "Doth our law judge any man, before it hear him, and know what he doeth?" (John 7:51), which drew the exasperated retort, "Are thou also of Galilee?" Nicodemus may not have been from Galilee but we know (John 3:1–21) that he had been secretly instructed by Jesus in the gospel. He would later bring a mixture of myrrh and aloes to dress the body of Jesus after the crucifixion, a very public act at a very dangerous time.

Although Nicodemus was probably a historical person, for John he became a prototype of those Pharisees living in the darkness (he secretly met with and questioned Jesus at night) who gradually came into the light.

28. Reading: Matthew 27

Answer: (b) "When he was set down on the judgment seat, his **wife** sent unto him, saying, Have thou nothing to do with that just man, for I have suffered many things this day in a dream because of him" (Matt 27:19).

All four gospels portray Pilate as reluctant to execute Jesus. In recent years some critics have tried to interpret this as an attempt by the later Christians to ingratiate themselves with Roman society by casting blame for the death of Jesus solely on the Jews. This glosses over the fact that Matthew's gospel was written specifically *to* the Jews, and here it is not only Pilate but even his wife who regard Jesus as innocent. In fact, it is only in Matthew that Pilate washes his hands of the matter—no matter how unlikely it would have been for a Roman governor to perform a Jewish ritual of absolution for a murder, as required by Deuteronomy 21:6–7: "And the elders of that city that are next unto the slain man shall wash their hands . . . and they shall answer and say, Our hands have not shed this blood, neither have our eyes seen it."

29. Reading: John 11

Answer: (a) Far from being villainous, the Jewish rulers are portrayed in John as genuinely distressed that Jesus' popularity will lead to a revolt against Rome and the destruction of the Jewish nation. **Caiaphas,** the high priest, presents the case (John 11:50) that it is better "that one man should die for the people, and that the whole nation perish not."

30. Reading: John 20

Answer: (c) "But **Thomas,** one of the twelve, called Didymous [twin, another of Jesus' nicknames] was not with them when Jesus came" (John 20:24). And, of course, what follows is the story of Doubting Thomas, whose skepticism isn't resolved until Jesus at a second appearance invites him to touch his wounds for himself.

WHAT AND WHY

31. Reading: Matthew 2
Answer: (a) "But when he heard that Archelaus did reign in Judaea in the room of his father Herod, he was afraid to go thither; notwithstanding, being warned of God in a dream, he turned aside into the parts of **Galilee**" (Matt 2:22). Herod I was a native of Idumea and therefore a foreign ruler of the Jews, which made him pathologically suspicious of his subjects. He murdered his wife Mariamne for no other reason than she, as a Maccabean, had a better claim to the throne than he did, and that same reasoning led to the executions of his two sons by her. The slaughter of the innocents would have been characteristic of him. At his death, the Romans decided to disperse power among his remaining sons: Herod Archelaus was given Judaea, Samaria, and Idumea; Herod Philip was given some smaller territories; and Herod Antipas was given Galilee and Perea. Apparently Antipas had a reputation as more easygoing than his brother Archelaus, which is why Joseph made his way to Galilee. On Archelaus' death in A.D. 6, Judaea became a directly controlled Roman province.

32. Reading: Luke 2, Leviticus 12
Answer: (b) Mary and Joseph offered as a sacrifice **a pair of turtledoves** (Luke 2:24). This passage is crucial to an understanding of the material circumstances of the Holy Family. Some have claimed that, as a carpenter, Joseph was a skilled craftsman or artisan, and argued that his independence and the fact he was neither an agricultural worker nor fisherman therefore placed the family in the middle class. The Law, as stated in Leviticus 12, for the ritual cleansing after the birth of a child tends to contradict this assertion, since the requirement was for a young lamb to be sacrificed and only if the mother "be not able to bring a lamb, then she shall bring two turtles or two young pigeons . . ." (Lev 12:8). It appears that Mary could not afford a lamb, since she presented only two

turtledoves. This fits with Mary's own words in the Magnificat, which seem unlikely from the young wife of a prosperous husband: "He hath put down the mighty from their seats, and exalted them of low degree. He hath filled the hungry with good things; and the rich he hath sent empty away" (Luke 1:52–53).

33. Reading: Matthew 2
   Answer: (c) "And he came and dwelt in a city called Nazareth: that it might be fulfilled which was spoken by the prophets, **He shall be called a Nazarene**" (Matt 2:23). There is no such prophecy in the Old Testament. Some scholars speculate that Matthew may have confused Judges 13:5, where the angel tells Hannah that her child Samuel "shall be a Nazarite unto God from the womb, and he shall begin to deliver Israel out of the hand of the Philistines." This seems implausible, as Matthew could not have been unaware of the Nazarite tradition that included two such famous figures as Samson and Samuel. Another possibility is that he was quoting from an oral tradition or from a book of the Old Testament that has been lost.

34. Reading: Matthew 4
   Answer: (d) Satan didn't offer Jesus **the Throne** because he couldn't.

35. Reading: Matthew 8
   Answer: (d) The **unclean spirit** cried, "I know thee who thou art, the Holy One of God" (Mark 1:24), just before Jesus cast him out. Throughout Mark, it is the demons who immediately recognize Jesus as the Messiah.

36. Reading: John 2
   Answer: (d) At a marriage feast at Cana, the host ran out of wine. "And when they wanted wine, the **mother of Jesus** saith unto him, They have no wine. Jesus saith unto her, Woman, what have I to do with thee? mine hour is not yet come. His mother saith unto the servants, Whatsoever he saith unto you, do it" (John 2:3–5). And sure enough, Jesus turned six pots of water into wine, and not just wine but "good wine."

This is one of the most discussed passages in the New Testament, and it can be read on many levels. On a human psychological level, Jesus' sharp words to Mary seem to reflect the impatience of a young man at a mother's natural pride. (How many other young and even adult men have been embarrassed by a mother's proud statements to her friends!) But the scholar A. Feullet warns against such worldly interpretation: "His detached attitude and his apparent hardness regarding Mary . . . should not be interpreted according to the laws governing ordinary human psychology [but as] a sign of the absolute transcendence of Jesus." Even so, modern readers are taken aback by his seemingly curt form of address to Mary as "Woman." In John 19:26, he will again use this form of address when, in his last act from the cross, he bids his disciple John to take care of Mary; he begins by saying to her, "Woman, behold thy son!" Rather than dismissive, the use of "Woman" seems here to be honorific, and many interpreters see its use as symbolic of Mary as the prototype of the mothering Church.

The turning of the water into wine has a rich symbolic meaning of its own, for as water was used under the Old Covenant for ritual purification, under the New Covenant wine will become the blood of Christ for the redemption of souls.

37. Reading: John 4
Answer: (a) "For thou hast had **five husbands;** and he whom thou now hast is not thy husband . . ." (John 4:6). This is a remarkable passage, not only because John devotes more space to this single conversation with a disreputable Samaritan woman than he does even to the call of the first disciples, but also because Jesus singles out this one woman to state explicitly for the first time who he is. In Matthew and Mark, Jesus is at some pains in the beginning of his ministry to quiet speculation over his true identity. Even in John when one of the first disciples, Nathanael, proclaims to Jesus "Rabbi, thou art the Son of God; thou art the King of Israel" (John 1:49), Jesus replies obliquely. He even reprimands his mother at Cana when she asks for his intervention, saying, "mine hour is not yet come" (John 2:4). But when the woman at the well says to Jesus that, when the Messiah comes, "he will tell us all things," Jesus replies, "I that speak unto thee am he."

38. Reading: Matthew 12:1–14; Mark 3:1–6; Luke 6:1–11; John 5:1–16

Answer: (b) Because **he healed on the Sabbath,** "the Pharisees went out, and held a council against him, how they might destroy him" (Matt 12:14). The Synoptics give as the cause of the dispute a man with a withered hand whom Jesus healed. John says it was an "impotent man"—a paralytic?—and the dispute erupted when the healed man was seen carrying his bed on the Sabbath and, when accosted for breaking the Law, replied, "He that made me whole, the same said unto me, Take up thy bed, and walk" (John 5:11). For the Pharisees, the precise regulation of the Sabbath requirements was symbolic of the entire Law, and therefore the slightest diminution of the Sabbath was a crack in the Law which could conceivably cause the entire structure to collapse. To Jesus the structure was hollow, and the rigor with which the Sabbath was regulated only symbolized the emptiness of faith within.

39. Reading: John 6

Answer: (a) When Jesus said, "Except ye eat the flesh of the Son of man, and drink his blood, ye have no life in you" and **"Whoso eateth my flesh, and drinketh my blood, hath eternal life"** and "He that eateth my flesh, and drinketh my blood, dwelleth in me, and I in him" (John 6: 53–56), many of his disciples said, "This is a hard saying; who can hear it?" John reports that "From that time many of his disciples went back, and walked no more with him" (John 6:66).

40. Reading: John
Answers:
a. I am the *bread* of life (6:35).
b. I am the *light* of the world (8:12).
c. I am the *door* of the sheep (10:7).
d. I am the good *shepherd* (10:11).
e. I am the *resurrection*, and the life (11:25).
f. I am the way, the *truth,* and the life (14:6).
g. I am the true *vine* (15:1).

THE BEATITUDES

41. Reading: Matthew 5
a. Blessed are the *poor in spirit:* for theirs is the kingdom of heaven.
b. Blessed are they that *mourn:* for they shall be comforted.
c. Blessed are the *meek:* for they shall inherit the earth.
d. Blessed are they which *hunger and thirst for righteousness:* for they shall be filled.
e. Blessed are the *merciful:* for they shall obtain mercy.
f. Blessed are the *pure in heart:* for they shall see God.
g. Blessed are the *peacemakers:* for they shall be called the children of God.
h. Blessed are they which are persecuted for righteousness' sake: for theirs is the kingdom of heaven.
i. Blessed are ye, when *men shall revile you,* and persecute you, and shall say all manner of evil against you falsely, for my sake.
j. Rejoice and be exceeding glad: for great is *your reward in heaven:* for so persecuted they the prophets which were before you.

THE SERMON ON THE MOUNT: MATTHEW 5–7

42. Ye are the light *of the world* (5:14).

43. And if thy right eye offend thee, *pluck it out* (5:29).

44. But whosoever shall smite thee on thy right cheek, *turn to him the other also* (5:39).

45. And whosoever shall compel thee to go a mile, *go with him twain* (5:41).

46. But lay up for yourselves treasures *in heaven* (6:20).

47. Ye cannot serve God *and mammon* (6:24).

48. Which one of you by taking thought can add *one cubit unto his stature* (6:27)?

49. Sufficient unto the day is the *evil thereof* (6:34).

50. Judge not, that *ye be not judged* (7:1).

51. Neither cast ye your pearls *before swine* (7:6).

52. Ask, and it *shall be given you* (7:7).

53. What man is there of you, whom if his son ask bread, will he give him *a stone* (7:9)?

54. Whatsoever ye would that men should do to you, do *ye even so to them* (7:12).

55. Ye shall know them by *their fruits* (7:16).

56. Therefore whosoever heareth these sayings of mine, and doeth them, I will liken him unto a wise man, which built *his house upon a rock* (7:24).

THE PARABLES

57. Reading: Matthew 24–30
Answer: (a) The enemy **sowed weeds.** This is Jesus' explanation why evil men seem to flourish and prosper in the world, for the husbandman decided to let the weeds and the wheat grow together until the harvest, when they would be separated and the weeds burned.

58. Reading: Matthew
Answer: (d) Jesus never likened the kingdom of heaven to a **camel,** but given his gift with metaphoric language, no doubt he could have.

59. Reading: Matthew 20: 1–16
Answer: (b) **All were paid equally,** meaning that it is never too late.

60. Reading: Matthew 21: 33–41
Answer: (b) **They killed the son.** This parable is not only a forecast of his own death, but a condemnation of the Jews for not properly tending to the Covenant.

61. Reading: Matthew 25:1–13
Answer: (c) The foolish virgins had not prepared for the bridegroom's coming by **getting oil for their lamps.**

62. Reading: Matthew 25: 14–30
Answer: (b) Jesus condemned **the man who did not use his talent.** A *talent* of silver in Jesus' time was worth about 3,000 shekels, which was an enormous amount of money when one considers that a shekel was worth about a day's wages. The etymology of the word in modern English usage descends directly from this parable: our modern word comes to us from the Old English *talente,* which is from the Latin *talentum,* which is the unit of money referred to by Jesus. It has long been a popular subject from the pulpit to equate the use of the *talents* in this parable with the use of our God-given talents, and from the point of view of the English language the equation is literally true.

63. Reading: Luke 16:19–31
Answer: (a) "And he said unto him, If they hear not Moses and the prophets, **neither will they be persuaded, though one rose from the dead**" (Luke 16:31).

64. Reading: Luke 18: 1–8
Answer: (b) The judge gave in just to stop the widow's **constant importuning.** If such persistence could sway an unjust judge, said Jesus, how much more could God be swayed by constant prayer?

Answers to CHAPTER 7:

"THE APOSTOLIC WRITINGS"

≈≈≈

page 122

MEMORABLE COMMENTS

1. Reading: Acts 10

Answer: (a) "Then Peter opened his mouth and said, Of a truth I perceive that God **is no respecter of persons**" (Acts 10:34).

2. Reading: 2 Corinthians 12:1–10

Answer: (b) ". . . there was given to me **a thorn in the flesh . . .**" (2 Cor 12:7). Paul "besought the Lord thrice" that this infirmity which was "a messenger of Satan to buffet me" might depart. The speculation over what this infirmity was has ranged from the medical to the psychological to the sexual to everything in between. It seems to have been chronic, although Paul prayed for relief only three times.

3. Reading: 1 Timothy 6

Answer: (c) This may be the most misquoted phrase in Scripture. In his letter to Timothy (6:10), Paul says it is the **love of money**—not money itself—**that is the root of all evil.**

4. Reading: James 5

Answer: (b) James implored the Christian community to wait for the coming of the Lord, saying, "Ye have heard of **the patience of Job**" (Jas 5:11). Considering what Job went through, this could not have been a comforting allusion.

5. Reading: Hebrews 13

Answer: (a) "Be not forgetful to entertain strangers: for thereby **some have entertained angels unawares**" (Heb 13:7).

6. Reading: 1 Corinthians 15

Answer: (b) "Behold, I shew you a mystery; We shall not all sleep, but we shall all be changed, In a moment, **in the twinkling of an eye,** at the last trump: for the trumpet shall sound, and the dead shall be raised incorruptible, and we shall be changed" (1 Cor 15:51–52). This is one of those beautiful phrases Handel selected for his *Messiah*.

7. Reading: Acts 9:1–9

Answer: (a) When Saul asked, "Who art thou, Lord," the reply came: "I am Jesus whom thou persecutest: it is hard for thee **to kick against the pricks**" (Acts 9:5). A rebellious horse or beast of burden who tries unsuccessfully to rebel kicks against the goads or spurs. In other words, Saul may have been trying to suppress an uncomfortable feeling about his persecution of the disciples or ignore the first stirrings of belief in the phenomenal news of Jesus' Resurrection. Christ is telling Saul that it is hard to resist the goading of the Spirit.

8. Readings: Romans 13

Answer: (b) "Let every soul be subject unto the higher powers. For there is no power but of God: **the powers that be** are ordained of God" (Rom 13:1). For a subversive and even revolutionary new doctrine, Christianity was unusually conservative, and Paul was the most conservative of all. Even when he rebuked the Sanhedrin after being slapped by the high priest's servants (Acts 23:5), he was appalled to discover he had just denounced the high priest himself, and in embarrassment quoted the Law, "Thou shalt not speak evil of the ruler of thy people" (Exod 22:28).

9. Reading: Acts 17

Answer: (a) The Jews in Thessalonia said of Paul and Silas that "these who have **turned the world upside down** have come hither also; whom Jason hath received . . ." (Acts

17:6). It was quite a compliment to Paul and Silas and the other Christian missionaries that their efforts over such a short period could be characterized as upending the entire world. "The World Turned Upside Down" became the refrain of a well-known song. In 1781 the British band struck it up as Lord Cornwallis surrendered to George Washington.

10. Reading: Acts 26

Answer: (c) ". . . Festus said with a loud voice, Paul, thou art beside thyself; **much learning doth make thee mad**" (Acts 26:24). The practical Romans had little use for book-learning, and the disputes among the Jews over the finer points of Mosaic Law must have confounded them.

FAMOUS PEOPLE (AND SOME THAT OUGHT TO BE)

11. Reading: Acts 1

Answer: (c) "And they gave forth their lots; and the lot fell upon **Matthias;** and he was numbered with the eleven disciples" (Acts 1:26). The "lots" could have been ballots, which would mean Matthias was elected. But more typically a lot was a kind of counter by which a question was decided. And in the preceding sentence, the disciples asked the Lord to show which of the two candidates he had chosen. The use of lots in trying to determine the will of God was not unusual in Israel, especially in earlier times. In Exodus, the high priest was instructed to wear the Urim and Thummim, which are thought to have been containers for the lots that would answer yes or no, indicating whether divine approval was given or withheld (see Exod 28:30).

12. Reading: Acts 5:1–11

Answer: (c) When Ananias and Sapphira were separately questioned, each lied and **each was struck dead.** The harshness of the punishment may not seem to fit the crime, but there is no doubt it had an effect on the community. "And great fear came upon all the church, and upon as many as heard these things" (Acts 5:11).

13. Reading: Acts 5:12–42

Answer: (a) The rabbi **Gamiliel,** grandson of the great rabbi Hilliel and teacher of Saul, offered words of advice that should be remembered during the religious wars that seem a plague on the world up to our time: "Refrain from these men, and let them alone: for if this counsel or this work be of men, it will come to nought: But if it be of God, ye cannot overthrow it; lest haply ye be found even to fight against God" (Acts 5:38–39).

14. Reading: Acts 7

Answer: (b) **Stephen,** one of the Greek-speaking deacons appointed by the disciples, was stoned to death. Saul was a witness.

15. Reading: Acts 8: 5–25

Answer: (a) **Simon,** more well known as Simon Magus through the ages, was a magician in Samaria when he converted. Evidently, though, the conversion was a trick: Simon seems to have been principally interested in how the disciples performed miracles through the Holy Spirit. When he saw this power came through the laying on of hands by the apostles, he made his bid for the office. This crime has been known since as *simony.*Many stories about Simon Magus that circulated in the second century indicated he persisted in magic and, in trying to outdo the Christians, became the first heretic.

16. Reading: Acts 5:26–40

Answer: (b) The **eunuch,** treasurer to the Candace of Ethiopia, had come to Jerusalem to worship. Candace was a hereditary title for the female ruler of the kingdom of Meroe, which was not in modern Ethiopia proper, but along the southern Nile. That such a high official as the treasurer practiced Judaism attests to the long-standing tradition that parts of this region were converted as far back as Solomon's reign. As noted previously, the ruling family of Ethiopia before the revolution claimed to be descended from Solomon, and the emperor carried the honorific "Lion of Judah."

17. Reading: Acts 9: 1–19
Answer: (c) **Ananias.** He was one of three men in Acts to bear this name, which means "Yahweh has been gracious."

18. Reading: Acts 12
Answer: (c) "Now about that time Herod the king stretched forth his hands to vex certain of the church. And he killed **James the brother of John** with the sword" (Acts 12:1–2). This Herod, known as Herod Agrippa I, was the grandson of Herod the Great, who grew up in Rome and secured the throne of Galilee by his friendship with Caligula and extended it to include Judea by his friendship with Claudius. To maintain some control over his fractious domain, he was scrupulous in his adherence to Mosaic Law. He executed James—the first of the original twelve disciples to be martyred—and imprisoned Peter because "it pleased the Jews," who had been unsuccessful in dealing with the new sect through the religious courts.

19. Reading: Acts 12
Answer: (b) This John "whose surname was Mark" is thought to be the same **John Mark** who accompanied Paul and Barnabus and who was the author of the gospel. However, it should be noted that the Hebrew name *John* and the Roman name *Mark* were about as common then as they are today.

20. Reading: Acts 13: 1–13
Answer: (a) The **sorcerer** Bar-jesus (son of Jesus) was attached to the court of Sergius Paulus, proconsul of Cyprus. It seems to have been a common practice of the time to employ magicians to read omens, although Bar-jesus didn't show much foresight in confronting Paul.

21. Reading: Acts 16: 11–5
Answer: (c) **Lydia** seems not to have been used as a proper name at this time, but refers to the kingdom of Lydia in Asia Minor, which was known for its quality dyes. The woman referred to by her homeland in this passage was probably an exporter to Macedonia. So Paul's first convert in Europe was probably not a European at all. The first European convert was

—take your pick—the centurion at the foot of the cross who proclaimed "Surely this was the Son of God!" (Matt 27: 54), the centurion Cornelius "of the band called the Italian band" converted by Peter, or the jailor at Philipi. (Some scholars have credited the speed of Christianity's expansion in the post-Apostolic period to the early conversions of Roman officers, who in their postings around the Empire and in Rome itself spread the gospel.)

22. Reading: Acts 16: 16–40
Answer: (b) Paul **cast the demon out of a soothsayer.** Magicians and fortune-tellers populate Acts as they must have populated the Mediterranean region, and the author seems to believe in them as much as the people do.

23. Reading: Acts 17: 15–34
Answer: (c) Athens under Roman rule had lost all semblance of political power, but retained enormous prestige as a center of learning and philosophy, and young men from the best families in Rome were expected to study there. The city was governed in these matters and in its internal affairs by a council which sat on the Areopagus or hill of Ares (Mars' hill). That Paul was invited to speak there shows the freedom of inquiry that characterized Athenian discourse, and that he was largely unsuccessful, owing to the doctrine of the Resurrection, should not be surprising among an audience composed of pagan philosophers. However, Paul had one notable success, and it was a major one, for to convert so prominent a figure as an Aeropagite, or **member of the Athenian council,** to the new faith would have had a tremendous impact. Tradition from the second century holds that Dionysius was the first bishop of Athens. If so, his prestige was such as to create a line of bishops by that name, for we know the bishop of Corinth in A.D. 173 was also Dionysius, and that in A.D. 250 another bishop by the same name was sent to Gaul as a missionary. This latter Dionysius became the patron saint of France under the Gallicized version of his name, St. Denis, which later tradition was to confuse with Dionysius the Aeropagite.

24. Reading: Acts 26

Answer: (d) "Then **Agrippa** said unto Paul, Almost thou persuadest me to be a Christian" (Acts 26:28). This Agrippa is Herod Agrippa II, the only son of Herod Agrippa, who, at his father's death, was appointed king over parts of his kingdom by Claudius. Exegesists are divided over whether Agrippa's comment was meant to be sincere or ironic, and that was probably exactly what Agrippa intended them to be.

25. Reading: Acts 28: 1–11

Answer: (a) The miracle of the poisonous **viper** had a great effect upon the people, and the bay into which the ship came for harbor after its arduous journey is known today as St. Paul's Bay.

26. Reading: Acts 18: 1–17

Answer: (b) **Sosthenes** was "chief ruler of the synagogue" (Acts 18:17), who was beaten after Paul was acquitted in Corinth of accusations by the Jews. It must be that the Jews considered Sosthenes a traitor, and he may have defended Paul at the trial before the proconsul. A few paragraphs earlier (18:8), Crispus is also described as chief ruler of the synagogue. He converted and must have lost his position as a result. Sosthenes was his replacement. To lose the second head of the synagogue in the space of eighteen months to this Christian heresy must have been more than the outraged Jews could bear. Sosthenes was the logical person then to write a joint letter with Paul to the new Christian congregation in Corinth, since most of its members were his former congregants.

27. Reading: 1 Corinthians 1, 3; Acts 18: 24–28

Answer: (a) **Apollos** "taught diligently the things of the Lord, knowing only the baptism of John" (Acts 18:25). More than a quarter century after his death, there were still disciples of John the Baptist. So Paul was essentially saying that the Church was divided unto factions: the Gentiles who followed him; the Jews who followed Peter and the original apostles; new Christians who had come over from the sect following John, and whom we might regard as fundamentalists, i.e., those who paid no heed to the leadership of Paul or Peter but adhered to their own understanding of the words of Jesus himself.

Apollos and Barnabus, because they left no writings, are two of the most underrated missionaries of the early Church. Apollos was obviously as well schooled in the Scriptures as Paul and made a great impression by his eloquence on the Jews. To Barnabus we owe the fact that Paul was received by the suspicious apostles after his conversion. No doubt his influence was due to his wealth: we know from Acts 4:36–37 that he was a landowner who contributed much to the apostles. It was Barnabus, too, who accompanied Paul to the Council of Jerusalem and there is no doubt that the esteem in which he was held helped in convincing the apostles of the necessity of Paul's mission to the Gentiles, a mission in which he played a substantial role.

28. Reading: Hebrews 5, 7

Answer: (c) Because **Melchizedek** is so briefly mentioned in Genesis, with no antecedents or explanation given, the tradition arose that he had no mother or father, but was a kind of eternal figure. His title, king of Salem, was also taken not to be the real title of a real figure in history, but a figurative title as king of peace. The writer of Hebrews makes use of this tradition as well as Scripture as seeing him as a prefigurement of the Messiah, the prince of peace.

WHAT AND WHY

29. Reading: Acts 2

Answer: (b) "And they were all filled with the Holy Ghost, and began to **speak with other tongues,** as the Spirit gave them utterance" (Acts 2:4). Glossolalia (from the Greek for tongue, *glossa*) was a phenomenon of the early Church which was basically of two kinds: speaking in understandable languages, as in the Pentecost experience; and speaking in "unknown" or "new" or incomprehensible "tongues." Nowhere else in the New Testament does the speaker in tongues seem to be comprehensible, and when Paul in 1 Corinthians 12 lists speaking with tongues among the gifts of the Holy Spirit, he also includes as a separate category the ability to interpret those who speak in tongues. Since Paul's account precedes Luke's in Acts by several decades, some wonder whether the disciples at Pentecost were as intelligible as Luke makes them appear.

30. Reading: Acts 3
Answer: (b) Peter's famous answer to **the lame man** who begged him for alms was, "Silver and gold have I none; but such as I have I give thee. In the name of Jesus Christ rise up and walk" (Acts 3:6). Surely the most amazing thing about the Pentecost experience was the transformation of Simon Peter. He went from cowering to towering, from fecklessness to faith. Later as he confronted the conflicts of the growing religion, he wasn't so surefooted (see Paul's complaint about his wavering on circumcision in Galations 2), but at this moment he was truly first of the apostles: first to proclaim openly the good news of the Resurrection, first to demonstrate his faith by performing miracles, and first to defend the faith before the astonished Sanhedrin.

31. Reading: Acts 6: 1–8
Answer: (d) The divisions were not, as the passage seems to state, between Greeks and Hebrews but between those who spoke Aramaic and those who spoke Greek (all were Jews), and this might also imply a little class bias, since not to be conversant in Greek at that time revealed provincialism and lack of education. But the real problem was a happy one: the Christian community was growing beyond its narrow Galilean origins to attract many of the more cosmopolitan Jerusalemites, and it had simply become too much for the apostles to **minister to the broader community's daily needs.**

32. Reading: Acts 10
Answer: (b) Here glossolalia, or **speaking in tongues,** was a sure sign that the Gentiles had been filled with the Holy Spirit, and it led Peter to ask of his colleagues, "Can any man forbid water, that these should not be baptized, which have received the Holy Ghost as well as we?" (Acts 10:47). This may be *the* pivotal moment in the history of Christianity as a world

religion, for when in the next verse Peter commands the Gentiles to be baptized, the new religion decisively breaks with the old.

33. Reading: Acts 11
Answer: (d) "And the disciples were called Christians first in **Antioch**" (Acts 11:26). Antioch was the capital of the Roman province of Syria, and one of the most important trade centers of the Empire. According to tradition, the name applied to the new religion was meant to be neither derogatory nor complimentary; it was simply bureaucratic. With so many sects and cults in their flourishing city to keep track of, and with this new religion attracting both Jews and Gentiles, city officials came up with the term "Christian" as a way of distinguishing it so they could keep track of it.

34. Reading: Acts 12: 20–23
Answer: (a) Psalm 115 begins with "Non nobis, Domine"—Not unto us, O Lord, but unto thy name give glory—which became one of the great hymns of the Middle Ages and was, tradition tells us, sung by Henry V's soldiers after his astonishing victory over the French at Agincourt. Herod, struck dead for having **blasphemed,** would have done well to have kept the psalm in mind.

35. Reading: Acts 15: 1–35
Answer: (c) The apostles seemed to have already made up their mind—favorably—on the matter of Gentiles. "But there rose up certain of the sect of the **Pharisees** which believed, saying, That it was needful to circumcise them, and to command them to keep the law of Moses" (Acts 15:5). Peter, in characteristic fashion, seemed to get worked up a bit in his reply to these Pharisaic interlopers, and ended by denouncing the Law altogether as "a yoke . . . which neither our fathers nor we were able to bear." This was strong stuff for a Jew to hear, much less to say.

36. Reading: Acts 15: 36–41
Answer: (b) Why **John Mark deserted Paul in Pamphylia** is one of the mysteries of Acts. It could have been

simple homesickness. It could have been a dispute over doctrine, such as the baptism of Gentiles. Acts 13:13 is silent on the question. But the evidence of Acts 15: 38–39 implies a lack of fortitude on John Mark's part.

The fact that John Mark is mentioned so often in Acts, even over such trivial matters, may mean that his gospel was already well known at the time of Luke's writing this account, and therefore he was a famous figure among Christians. (We know from Colossians 4:10 that he and Paul were reconciled, and he is mentioned favorably two other times in Paul's epistles.)

37. Reading: Acts 16: 16–40

Answer: (c) Paul's self-assurance and command are nowhere more evident than in his refusal to flee when an earthquake shattered the prison in which he and Silas were being kept. Obviously impressed, the jailor **converted** on the spot.

38. Reading: Acts 18: 12–17

Answer: (b) The Roman mind was logical and practical, and it had no patience with anything theoretical and impractical. That placed **theology** beyond its remotest reaches, and Christianity—with its paradoxes and otherworldliness—might as well have been from another planet. Like Pontius Pilate, like Festus, like Felix and all the many Roman officials to come over the next three hundred years as Christianity bloomed like a huge subterranean flower, Gallio effectively washed his hands of the matter.

39. Reading: Acts 18: 18

Answer: (b) Paul seemed to have taken a Nazarite vow as provided under the Law in Numbers 6:1–23. The word *Nazarite* comes from *nadhar*, "to vow," hence, "a person who has made a vow." The Law set the terms and conditions for such a vow, which in most cases was for a period of thirty days, and required that the vower not drink wine, **cut his hair,** or touch a dead body. We know of two instances—Samson and Samuel—when the vow was made at birth and in perpetuity, and John the Baptist may have been a perpetual Nazarite also.

Paul would have shaven his head in preparation for the vow, so that he would not have to cut his hair as it grew, and the shaven hair would be presented at the Temple when the term of the vow was over. Thus Paul said in rejecting his friends' invitation to stay longer in Ephesus, "I must by all means keep this feast that cometh in Jerusalem . . ." (Acts 18:21).

For what purpose Paul made this vow, Luke does not say and probably did not know. However, it does show that the great missionary to the Gentiles was himself a strict observer of the Jewish tradition in which he was raised.

40. Reading: Acts 19: 23–41

Answer: (a) ". . . this Paul hath persuaded and turned much people, saying that **they be no gods, which are made with hands**" (Acts 19:26). Ephesus was a major tourist attraction, owing to the magnificent temple of Diana, or Artemis, the Artemision, one of the Seven Wonders of the World, first constructed in 550 B.C. by Croesus, the fabulously wealthy king of Lydia, and finally destroyed by Goth invaders in A.D. 262. Ephesus was chosen as its site because of "the image which fell down from Jupiter" (19:35), no doubt a meteor which was seen as a heavenly portent. Paul's radical new doctrine (which in fact was nothing more than a restatement of the Second Commandment's prohibition against graven images) threatened the tourist trade and the silversmiths who profited from it.

41. Reading: Acts 20: 6–12

Answer: (a) ". . . as Paul was long preaching, he sunk down with sleep, and **fell down from the third loft,** and was taken up dead." Anyone who has fallen asleep during a long sermon can have nothing but sympathy for Eutychus.

42. Reading: Acts: 21

Answer: (b) Agamus had correctly predicted the worldwide drought under Claudius which had impoverished Judaea for three years (Acts 11:27), so his warning that **the Jewish authorities would arrest Paul** was not to be taken lightly.

43. Reading: Acts 22–24
Answer: (c) "He hoped also that **money should have been given him** of Paul, that he might loose him . . ." (Acts 24:26). This time-honored custom of the Roman government was ignored by Paul.

PAUL'S BEST LINES

44. It is more blessed to give than *to receive*.

45. The wages of sin is *death*.

46. Be not overcome of evil, but overcome evil *with good*.

47. It is better to marry than *to burn*.

48. I am made all things to *all men*.

49. For now we see through a glass darkly, but then *face to face*.

50. O death, where is *thy sting*?

51. God loveth a *cheerful giver*.

52. Let us not be weary in *well doing*.

53. Labour of *love*.

54. The day of the Lord so cometh as a *thief* in the night.

55. We brought nothing into this world, and it is certain we can carry *nothing out*.

56. I have fought the *good fight*.

57. I have kept *the faith*.

REVELING IN REVELATION

58. Reading: Revelation 1

Answer: (a) "I was in the Spirit **on the Lord's day** . . ." (Rev 1:10). This is the first unambiguous reference in Christian literature to the day of the Resurrection—that is, Sunday—as a special day.

59. Reading: Revelation 2–3

Answer: (c) In an apt metaphor, John writes of the church at **Laodicea,** "So then because thou art lukewarm, neither cold nor hot, I will spue thee out" (Rev 3:16).

60. Reading: Revelation 4

Answer: (b) The four beasts—the lion, the calf, the beast with the face of a man, and the eagle—have traditionally been identified with the four Gospels: the lion as Matthew (for royalty), the calf or young bull with Mark (for power), the face of the man with Luke (for wisdom), and the eagle with John (for divinity). John did not see a **lamb** at the Throne of God.

61. Reading: Revelation 5

Answer: (b) **The Lamb had seven horns and seven eyes,** which John says represent "the seven Spirits of God sent forth into all the earth" (Rev 5:6). The number seven, which plays such an important part in John's revelation, attained its symbolic importance in Jewish and Christian numerology from the first account of Creation in Genesis. The division of the month into weeks, and the week into seven days—which was unknown to the Romans, who divided the month into two slightly uneven fortnights—may have derived from the fact that there are seven visible heavenly bodies which move independently against the panoply of the heavens: the sun, the moon, Mercury, Venus, Mars, Jupiter, and Saturn. From these we still retain some of our English names for the days of the week: Monday (moon-day) and Saturday (Saturn-day), for example. (Others are named after Norse deities.) In the Romance languages, all the days of the week retain the ancient Christian nomenclature.

62. Reading: Revelation 6
Answer: (a) The Four **Horsemen** of the Apocalypse
are the rider of the pale white horse holding a bow (Conquest),
the rider of the red horse (Slaughter), the rider of the black
horse (Famine), and the rider of the pale horse (Death).

63. Reading: Revelation 7–11
Answer: (c) The murder of the **two witnesses** may be
a reference to the executions of Peter and Paul in Rome under
Nero (as good a candidate as any for "the beast that ascendeth
out of the bottomless pit"). Some exegesists believe the "great
city" is Rome, and that the phrase "where also our Lord was
crucified" is an addition by a copyist who thought John surely
must have meant Jerusalem, which he well might have.

64. Reading: Revelation 12
Answer: (b) The **"woman clothed in the sun"** is
thought to be the Virgin Mary, the Church, or Israel—or all
three. Certainly artistic representations of the Virgin Mary have
made liberal use of the symbolism of this passage, including
the crown of twelve stars and the crushed serpent underneath
her feet. Thus the Virgin Mary becomes the "second Eve," but
this time the serpent loses. The vision of Our Lady of
Guadelupe continued the metaphor, and in fact the name
Guadelupe is Spanish for *Coat le lu pej*, which in Nahuatl means
"one who crushed the serpent."

65. Reading: Revelation 13
Answer: (a) "Here is wisdom. Let him that hath understanding count the number of the beast: for it is the number
of a man; and his number is **Six hundred threescore and six**"
(Rev. 13:18). The "number of a man" refers to the common
practice among the ancients of writing in a code based on as-
signing a number to letters of the alphabet. (Obviously the
Romans didn't have to work too hard at this; their numbers
were alphabetic letters: $V = 5$, $L = 50$, $C = 100$, etc.) John's Christian readers—those that "hath understanding"—would have
known, presumably, what code he is using. The most often
suggested candidate for the man based on such a code is the
emperor Nero. Nero Caesar in Greek is *Neron Caesar*, and if it is

then translated letter by letter to Hebrew, the number does indeed amount to 666. If this seems a rather complicated way of arriving at a solution, one must remember that many ancient and medieval numerologists, including the Jewish cabalists, spent their entire careers in trying to interpret mystical sayings through such codes.

Why was John writing in code? At the time Revelation was written, Domitian was emperor, and his policy was full persecution of the Christians as traitors. To identify a Caesar as such a great malefactor would be treasonous. Like many of the passages of the Book of Daniel under the persecution of Antiochus Epiphanes, much of Revelation is meant only for initiates who would understand its meaning.

Many Christian exegesists dispute that John was writing about events of his own time and hold that the number of the beast is a prophecy as yet unfulfilled.

66. Reading: Revelation 14
Answer: (d) "These are they which were not defiled with women; for they are **virgins**" (Rev 14:4). This can be taken literally, or in keeping with the common biblical metaphor in which sexual immorality represents idolatry; in other words, these are the ones who have stayed faithful to the Lord and "are without fault."

67. Reading: Revelation 17–18
Answer: (a) **Babylon** is thought to be a reference to Rome, the great persecutor, as when John hints to his readers: "And here is the mind which hath wisdom. The seven heads [of the beast on which the woman sits] are seven mountains, on which the woman sitteth" (Rev 17:9).

68. Reading: Revelation 19–21
Answer: (c) "And I John saw the holy city, new **Jerusalem**, coming down from God out of heaven, prepared as a bride adorned for her husband" (Rev 21:2).

BIBLIOGRAPHY
≈≈≈

The following is a selected bibliography which may also serve as a reading list for the reader interested in pursuing biblical studies. In general, these books are easily accessible to the non-scholar.

Alter, Robert. *The World of Biblical Literature.* New York: Basic Books, 1992. Our foremost literary critic on the Hebrew Bible.

Alter, Robert, and Frank Kermode, eds. *The Literary Guide to the Bible.* Cambridge: Harvard University Press, 1987. A collection of often brilliant essays on each of the books.

Archer, Gleason L. *A Survey of Old Testament Introduction.* Revised Edition. Chicago: Moody Press, 1964, rev. ed. 1974. Dense in parts, and argumentative in others, but in all a refreshing defense of the literalist position.

Asimov, Isaac. *Asimov's Guide to the Bible.* New York: Wings Books, 1988. Very helpful on points on geography, ancient peoples, intra-biblical references, and other difficulties the reader will encounter.

St. Augustine. *The City of God.* The Bishop of Hippo, ca. A.D. 400. Explores biblical matters such as why the patriarchs are said to have lived so long, with insights that are predictably fascinating.

Bloom, Harold. *The Book of J.* New York: Random House, 1990. An opinion on the Pentateuch, enthusiastically delivered.

Boa, Kenneth D., et al. *The New Open Bible, King James Version.* Nashville: Thomas Nelson Publishers, 1990. Contains over 100 informative essays, plus helpful diagrams and guides.

Cross, F. L., ed. *The Oxford Dictionary of the Christian Church.* New York: Oxford University Press, 1983.

Dockery, David S., ed. *Holman Bible Handbook.* Nashville: Holman Bible Publishers, 1992. A useful and well-designed guide from the Southern Baptist Convention. Reports the latest scholarship but carefully weighs the traditionalist view.

Erlich, Eugene, and Donald H. Scott. *Mene, Mene, Tekel.* New York: HarperCollins, 1990. The background and explanations of the best-known phrases in the Bible.

Freedman, David Noel, ed. *The Anchor Bible Dictionary.* New York: Doubleday, 1992. A monumental achievement in six volumes, without a doubt the best reference guide for any serious person interested in the Bible and recent scholarship about it.

Friedman, Richard Elliott. *Who Wrote the Bible?*

New York: Summit Books, 1987. More detail on the Pentateuch, aided by some educated guesses.

Frye, Northrup. *The Great Code: The Bible and Literature*. Orlando: Harcourt Brace Jovanovich, Publishers, 1983.

Greeley, Andrew M., and Jacob Neusner. *The Bible and Us*. New York: Warner Books, 1991. The novelist-priest and a rabbi probe their differences.

Jeffrey, David Lyle. *A Dictionary of Biblical Tradition in English Literature*. Grand Rapids: William B. Eerdmans Publishing Company, 1992. A valuable guide to the Bible's influence on our literary tradition.

Keller, Werner. *The Bible As History*. New York: William Morrow and Company, 1974. A basic introduction to biblical archeology, which is, unfortunately, somewhat dated even in its 1988 edition.

Kline, Meredith. *Treaty of the Great King*.

Lang, Stephen J. *The Complete Book of Bible Trivia*. Wheaton, IL: Tyndale Publishers, Inc., 1988. Great fun, and—without a doubt—it is complete.

Mears, Henrietta. *What the Bible Is All About*. Revised Edition. Ventura, CA: Regal Books, rev. ed. 1983. A romanticized viewpoint, which nevertheless contains some good points except when it obstinately refuses to look facts in the face.

Meier, John P. *A Marginal Jew: Rethinking the Historical Jesus*. New York: Anchor Bible Reference Library, Doubleday, 1991. An attempt to consider the scholarship neutrally.

Meredith, J. L. *Meredith's Book of Bible Lists*. Minneapolis, MN: Bethany House Publishers, 1980.

Price, Reynolds. *A Palpable God*. New York: Atheneum, 1978. Thirty stories from the Bible, translated by the author. But the introduction alone is worth the price of the book.

Russ, Daniel. "Exodus: Dwelling with Glory," *The Epic Cosmos*. Dallas, TX: The Dallas Institute Publications, 1992. An examination of the real meaning of myth.

Scroggie, W. Graham. *Scroggie's Bible Handbook*. Old Tappan, NJ: Fleming H. Revell Company, n.d. Full of insights, and brightly written.

Shanks, Hershel, et al. *The Dead Sea Scrolls After Forty Years*. Washington: Biblical Archaeology Society, 1991. A symposium on the latest finds.

Willington, H. L. *Willington's Book of Bible Lists*. Wheaton, IL: Tyndale House Publishers, 1987.

Also informative are the introductory essays in *The New Jerusalem Bible* (New York: Doubleday) and *The New American Bible* (New York: Catholic Book Publishing Company).

—W.A.

INDEX

≈≈≈